Friend or Foe: The Parado

Jenny Byast

Friend or Foe: The Paradox of Forming Strategic Alliances

Managerial Perceptions of Alliance Success - Demographic of managers that contribute to their decision making

Scholar's Press

Impressum / Imprint
Bibliografische Information der Deutschen Nationalbibliothek: Die Deutsche
Nationalbibliothek verzeichnet diese Publikation in der Deutschen
Nationalbibliografie; detaillierte bibliografische Daten sind im Internet über
http://dnb.d-nb.de abrufbar.
Alle in diesem Buch genannten Marken und Produktnamen unterliegen
warenzeichen-, marken- oder patentrechtlichem Schutz bzw. sind
Warenzeichen oder eingetragene Warenzeichen der jeweiligen Inhaber. Die
Wiedergabe von Marken, Produktnamen, Gebrauchsnamen, Handelsnamen,
Warenbezeichnungen u.s.w. in diesem Werk berechtigt auch ohne besondere
Kennzeichnung nicht zu der Annahme, dass solche Namen im Sinne der
Warenzeichen- und Markenschutzgesetzgebung als frei zu betrachten wären
und daher von jedermann benutzt werden dürften.

Bibliographic information published by the Deutsche Nationalbibliothek: The
Deutsche Nationalbibliothek lists this publication in the Deutsche
Nationalbibliografie; detailed bibliographic data are available in the Internet
at http://dnb.d-nb.de.
Any brand names and product names mentioned in this book are subject to
trademark, brand or patent protection and are trademarks or registered
trademarks of their respective holders. The use of brand names, product
names, common names, trade names, product descriptions etc. even without
a particular marking in this work is in no way to be construed to mean that
such names may be regarded as unrestricted in respect of trademark and
brand protection legislation and could thus be used by anyone.

Coverbild / Cover image: www.ingimage.com

Verlag / Publisher:
Scholar's Press
ist ein Imprint der / is a trademark of
OmniScriptum GmbH & Co. KG
Heinrich-Böcking-Str. 6-8, 66121 Saarbrücken, Deutschland / Germany
Email: info@scholars-press.com

Herstellung: siehe letzte Seite /
Printed at: see last page
ISBN: 978-3-639-51933-4

This book is dedicated to:

My friend and mentor Dr Azhdar Karami

&

The most inspiring woman I know

My friend Nicki Walker

Contents

Chapter 1 Introduction

1.1 Introduction

This book through empirical research explores the characteristics of manager's that influence their management decision making. An empirical study of owner mangers perceptions of the benefits of strategic management and in particular their strategic choices (Beverland and Bretherton, 2001; Persona et al, 2004; Brinckmann et al, 2010; Andersen 2011). The consequence of which may be them engaging with strategic alliances or other partnerships (Anslinger and Copeland, 1998; Baloh et al, 2008).

It explores the phenomena of management behaviour and decision making as the all pervasive influence on the business and to determine which of a managers characteristics (Cui and Mak, 2002; Carmen et al, 2006) might significantly influence their strategic management practices.

The study focuses on SMES in the High Tech sector in the UK. The owner managers are taken as the unit of analysis. The demographics and background characteristics of the managers' e.g. age, education and experience are used to determine how these might contribute to alliance success.

The specific characteristics of the firms e.g. size, age, location and particular industrial sector are possible determinants of strategic alliance success.

Statistical data about the formation of strategic alliances is not collated nor readily available. Evidence from sources such as the OECD (2005) suggests that SMEs generally and those in the high tech in particular are on the increase. This is due to the demand for more efficient and advanced technology. Alliances between major players are still newsworthy it is noted that more alliances are taking place between SMEs and these firms are prevalent in the computer and electronics industries.

Similarly, academic, policy makers and practitioner's interest in alliances has increased. SME owner's behaviour and characteristics have always been important in their strategic decision making nowadays they also feature in their decisions to include strategic alliances in their firm's survival strategy. This is evidenced by the wealth of literature published during the last decade (Pansiri, 2005; Pidduck, 2006; Gulati et al, 2009).

Strategic Alliances allow managers to form strategies with other firms to increase their core capabilities and their competitiveness. This book examines the use of decision making by small firms as part of their strategic management which may result in the employment of strategic alliances in the high tech sector in the UK. There is a focus on management demographics and background characteristics as a major influence on decision-making and engagement with strategic alliances. Based on the assumption that an individual's characteristics and prior experience will influence their propensity to undertake strategic management and be proactive in engaging in creating alliances.

Technology changes have increased the number of high tech firms entering the market this increased competition requires firms to be more competitive. Historically Porter (1996), raises the question of how firms can become more competitive when they may be

4

resource strained, this is still significant during the economic turbulence we are facing. In addition if they are unable to meet the technological change of pace they will not be able to compete with larger incumbent firms. The barriers therefore in some respects are higher for new entrants.

Furthermore a more sophisticated consumer means that product delivery and quality need to be improved, increasing the pressure on SMEs to be innovative and competitive.

Speculation that increased formalisation of strategic management and planning of firms activities will guide this transformation from research and development towards a marketing orientation and through the firms various life stages. Governments have long recognised the significant role of SMEs in the economy and have increased measures to support such firms an acknowledgement of their contribution to employment and economic regeneration through innovation and competition.

Due to the important role SMEs firms play in the innovation cycle governments are placing resources and support for these firms as high priority, combined with this is their potential to create new jobs and contribute to the economy. To do this the skills of the manager, SME competencies and the resource needs of the firm have to be audited and analysed with a view to strategically obtaining them. To carry out these important roles however firms have to be able to achieve high performance and be sustainable. Arguments in both literature and research proposes that firms need to be strategic and plan meanwhile other arguments propose that SMEs need to be flexible.

Whatever their stance policymakers, practitioners and researchers of SMEs need to be aware:

- of external and internal environments
- understand their customers
- have access to the knowledge and resources of their competitors

When the competition has resources that they cannot imitate, replicate or acquire through purchase strategic alliances are a preferred method of expansion for larger firms.

This could be considered a good strategic management option for the smaller firm. In finding these partners SMEs need to find an organisational fit. To do this according to Harrison (2003) they need to have similar aims and objectives with the organisations structure, business processes, cultures and systems

Having organisational fit combined with similar motivation for the strategic alliance will enable resource sharing, open communication and the achievement of goals. If organisational fit does not occur then conflict, breakdown of trust and a failed alliance may be the outcome.

Organisational fit will take into account management styles and their individual values (dominant logic) this reinforces the need to study managers at individual and firm levels Joshi et al (2010).

As motivation is an emotional response it cannot be measured without measuring individuals and their perceptions. The synergy that is needed for organisational fit may be difficult to find in SMEs as the cost in creating the synergy is greater than any benefits from creating and working on a strategic alliance. To perform these alliances successfully careful planning, monitoring and evaluation throughout the process is required.

As illustrated by Schumpeter (1939) when the firm begins to grow in size the need for specialists functions become apparent. At this stage there is a need for formalisation of planning and the utilisation of strategic management.

1.2 Research background

Throughout history it has been better to cooperate with other companies, nations and markets, this prevents adverse fluctuations, poor product development and products in the market that are out priced due to inflationary research and development costs.

During the most recent technological revolution, firms have acknowledged the positive outcomes when they cooperate either inter-firm or with multiple partners to develop up and down stream integration. This has provided better return for companies than mergers and acquisitions which frequently results in:

- one party with reduced power or assets
- through the appropriation of trade secrets by one of the firms
- information and intellectual property loss
- move on customers
- one of the firms embark on a hostile takeover.

Despite the above assumptions it is not clear how:

- businesses choose their partners,
- how outcomes are measured
- at what point the alliance can be considered a success or failure and how this impinges on undertaking future joint ventures or strategic alliances.

The industrial revolution supplied the business world with tools and mechanisms for production and distribution. In a similar way new technologies are providing the means for innovation, progress and an increase in products for a range of markets. The high tech industry is an umbrella term for many industries whose focus is either on the development of technologies or those that use the technology to design or develop their own products including the development of intangible core competencies (Joia and Malheiros, 2009). This study will be focusing on those under the Standard Industry Classification (SIC) codes associated with manufacturing.

Alliances between multinationals have been part of the historical landscape born out of a mutual need to share risks, reduce costs and reach firms' objectives (Smith, 2003). For larger competing firms it could mean the building of large new plants or heavy investment of capital. These shared risks forces the companies to commit to each other and despite being competitors in some markets they cooperate in others. These large global players have management and legal teams to seek out and brokerage alliances and to manage the successful selection and operation of those alliances. Despite this there are still reports of failure, dissatisfaction and the effects of rivalry outside the alliance are felt.

Small domestic SMEs on the other hand are of necessity more specialised in their activities and do not have the access to similar resources as larger firms. This increases the importance of efficient interaction with other firms and public research institutions for research and development (R&D), exchange of knowledge and, potentially, for commercialisation and marketing activities OECD (2005).

Despite this SME managers are less likely to entertain the idea of an alliance and shy away because of the implied cost in terms of resources needed to successfully form alliances and in particular those in the high tech industry. Traditionally scientists or inventors worked independently and were not schooled in management and lacked the skills to develop and market their products.

Teece (1986) states that in the high tech industries where the pace of change is fast and competition is high, these owner managers who remain resource poor and reliant on their core capabilities are not innovating or achieving goals or objectives. Therefore they need to recognise the need to cooperate with others despite not having the knowledge to undertake steps to form alliances Minshall et al, (2008) and therefore often becoming the subject of crisis management Herbane, (2010).

It has been argued that inter firm cooperation is an efficient way of increasing a firms capacity or competiveness, capturing new markets, increasing profits or elevating the status of some of the firms (Lorange and Roos, 1991a; O'Reilly and Finnegan, 2007; Smith, 2003; Chen and Karami, 2010; Lin and Lin, 2010; Shah and Swaminathan, 2008; Clarke-Hill et al, 2003; Lin et al, 2009).

Despite this assertion many small firms avoid forming relationships and if they do many fail. It is suggested that it is a lack of conscious planning of the alliance that causes this, as a result of this they may find them-selves taken advantage of by predatory firms disguised as friends.

There is evidence that an individual's demographics and background characteristics influences partner selection (Shah and Swaminathan, 2008; Chen and Karami, 2010) and promotes organisational learning (Das and Kumar, 2007; Eisner et al, 2009; Escriba-Esteve and Urra-Urbieta, 2002). What is less researched is how these firms should go about selecting a partner and what assists in the decision making (Minshall et al, 2008).

1.3 Strategic alliances for the 21st Century business environment

Prior studies have stated that firms have to be strategically managed, even those that are considered entrepreneurial, this is especially true for the need of inter-firm cooperation in any form it takes whether through sharing resources, knowledge or other activity. It is well documented that undertaking Strategic Alliances has increased over the last decades (Lorange and Roos, 1992; Das and He, 2006; Teng and Das, 2008) with some predicting (Marshall 2004) that this will require companies to become capable of creating and maintaining relationships necessary for alliances to be successful.

A number of factors are key drivers of this new type of business environment (Das and Kumar, 2010; Hitt et al, 2002). For example cheaper productivity from overseas results in markets being flooded with cheaper products. This is enabled by technological advances contributing to mass production at lower costs. These products satisfy domestic consumers, but cause problems for SMEs as they try to imitate the practices of larger established firms.

SMEs are resource strained and for some capabilities may be lacking in some areas for this reason and to remain competitive domestic SMEs need to produce quality products efficiently at lower cost as well as offering a product that is unique and different from the competitors. It is well documented that the majority of SMEs have limited resources and reduced capabilities, to address these shortcomings they need to consider working with other companies who have complementary resources (Hamel et al, 2002; Harrison, 2003; Lin et al, 2009; Das and Kumar, 2010).

Das and Teng (2000) talk about this collaborative advantage and have carried out a diverse range of research in a number of industries considering the use of strategic alliances at various stages of the process applying different methodologies. Building on this body of work Hoffmann and Schlosser (2001) assert that it will be beneficial to firms in gaining competitive advantage if they are able to successfully manage strategic alliances.

e.g. (Stuart, 1997) and conclude that many do not achieve the expected results due to their inability to manage the alliance due to lack of managerial experience and the inability to commit time and other resources to the alliance. There is also the perception from some that the alliance may be the opportunity for opportunistic firms to accumulate knowledge without supplying the required resource to the firm. Little empirical research has been conducted into why there is such a high failure rate when the expected outcome is success for both companies; furthermore, little examination is undertaken in to the perceived reason for failure.

It is important that as the number of SMEs increases that those who experience a positive alliance relationship also increase. Currently the correlation between strategic alliance involvement and success is negative and research is required to investigate how

11

this can be reversed. Through research and recording strategies that have provided positive experiences for managers it may be possible to minimise future risk (Mitsuhashi, 2002).

1.4 Prior researchers

There is copious research from academics, policy makers and practitioners around the themes of management characteristics and strategic management (Goll et al, 2008), strategy formulation and processes, management behaviour and decision making (Kauer et al, 2007) and alliances (Adobor, 2006). Pansiri (2005 pp 1097) combined "two streams of management literature (cognitive base and strategic alliances)" however there has been little integration from a research point of view to establish a link between management behaviour, decision making and the perceived success of alliances, empirical research has focused on team management and the effect on firms (Norburn and Birley, 1988; Pasanen and Laukkanen, 2006; Pegels and Yang, 2000).

Research focuses have been on management and alliance in terms of mergers and acquisitions, Joint ventures, measuring alliance performance (Lunnan and Haugland 2007), and strategic management planning (March and Gunasekaran, 1999). However there has been some development in creative alliances in recent years which have resulted in increased research into life cycles of alliances (Parker, 2000; Jarratt, 1998), analysis into their formation (Lin and Darling, 1999; Beverland and Bretherton, 2001), critical success factors for inter-firm cooperation (Chen and Karami, 2010) and the presentation of models for partner selection Sarkis et al, 2007) and finally the determinants of risks and benefits of alliances (Smith and Zahrly, 1993; Beverland and Bretherton, 2001)

It has been proposed by Ring (2000) that there is an emphasis on studying the governance of alliances and how this effects the alliance. Furthermore there is little understanding about the relationships within and between formal and informal processes. Lin and Darling (1999) suggest that more research should be done in the area of factors that facilitate or hamper strategic alliance formation and Doz (1996) argues that more research should be on processes of strategic alliances

Despite a wealth of research into strategic alliances some (Lewis, 1990; Doz, 1996; Lin and Darling, 1999; Das and Teng, 2000; Ireland et al, 2002; Iyer, 2002; Ring, 2002) suggest that there are still gaps in the academic literature including alliance formation and duration, factors contributing to success and failure. Studies have highlighted elements that influence strategic alliance formation and include such things as risk and success factors, uncertainty, resource allocation (Smith and Zahrly, 1993), knowledge transfer (Gravier et al, 2008), management (Carmen et al, 2006;)

Despite the wealth of literature and studies the reasons these gaps remain could be attributed to the fact that prior research has not concentrated on strategic alliance processes instead they have focused on the life cycle of an alliance. They have also used smaller samples of both the population and industry sectors.

In terms of decision-making in strategic alliance formation management behaviour, influence of their characteristics and prior experiences have on alliance engagement or avoidance has been neglected. As well as this omission they have not linked alliances in to the whole strategic planning of SMEs and either intentionally or unintentionally see them as being an add on rather than an integral part of their strategic planning. It would appear that strategic alliances are seen at best as necessary interlopers and at its worst as necessary for crisis management.

To address the gap in literature this study focuses on individual managers demographics and background characteristics such as age, education and prior experience exploring the impact on decision making and as a result its influence on alliance engagement as a strategic choice. This is done with a view to stressing the fact that alliances are or should be part of the strategic management of a firm and for this reason the view of this study is that managers make decisions about their environment and this informs how they are going to operate and determines strategic choices one of which is strategic alliances as opposed to going it alone.

The rational for choosing individual managers and not top management teams (TMT) is that these have already been extensively researched (Norburn and Birley, 1988; Pegels and Yang, 2000; Pansiri, 2005; Carmen et al, 2006; Pasanen and Laukkanen, 2006; Goll et al, 2008;) who have all reviewed the upper echelon theory with regards to managerial characteristics and their effect on firm performance. Sanyal and Guvenli (2004) carried out a study on individual managers however their focus was on the attributes and abilities expected of upper level managers in a three country study. As prior research has used the terms such as inter-firm cooperation, alliance, strategic alliance etc interchangeably this shortfall will also be addressed.

1.5 Rational for research

The rationale for this research is that the concept of SMEs in the high tech sector is changing and as can be seen in table 1.1 this has come about through a mixture of policy makers, academia and practitioners who acknowledge the contribution made to the economy by these firms.

Table 1.1   Historical and contemporary view of SMEs in the high tech sector

Historical	Contemporary
Historically the view was of firms working in isolation and who were wholly self-sufficient, these are essential characteristics for the protection of intellectual property.	Today firms need to be more strategic and to look outside the firm for resources to enable the reduction of their overheads and to acquire knowledge that is in the ownership of their competitors.
Historically sharing ideas with other firms would have been considered too high risk however more businesses are forming collaborations	Today small firms need to do more than survive they need growth strategies and long term planning and need to alter the focus of the firms as it grows from one of technological innovation to one who is focused on the market and the customer.

often with former competitors to enable them to survive.	These small firms need to align their strategies and to be aware of internal and external factors impacting on the business.
Little interference from policy makers, grouped together with other SMEs.	The recognition of the contribution to innovation by these smaller firms is recognised by policy makers and legislation is put in place to reduce bureaucracy faced by these firms.
Academia focused on larger firms in particular MNEs and the impact of global strategic alliances	Small firms in the high tech sector have become the focus on academia as it is recognised their contribution to the economy and the sheer volume of entrepreneurial firms despite the economic climate, questions include how do they survive, what tools do they use?

Source – Multiple Sources

As more companies choose cooperation over competition the question to be asked is what factors or criteria are important when a firm seeks out a partner and this is one area where theory and practice have not yet developed and there is a need to learn more to design out the possible failures that can occur or at the very least to minimise risk. To do this it is important to understand the demographics and background characteristics of the SME manager and what managers perceive to contribute to successful alliances and what they attribute to the cause of failure.

The study is interested in the managers of SMEs and their motivation for alliance activity. Therefore this study combines the two main approaches on collecting data on alliances found in the literature.

Previous researchers have;-

- either investigated the firms alliance activities which lead to innovative behaviour,

- Alternatively, they investigate the innovation that occurs as a result of the alliance if it has significantly affected the firms products or processes.

- Previous research has focused on one industry sector, this study is taking from a range that includes, nano-technology, biotechnology, telecommunications, software development, chemical, petrochemical, bio medical and other technology sectors (Smith and Zahrly, 1993) This enables observation of the dynamics of a range of industry types who will react and choose alliance partners differently (Lin et al, 2009).

This is partially because some are labour or capital intensive while others are technology intensive and as a result what they seek and what they have to offer will vary as will the managerial types to be found in these industries (Carment et al, 2006; Kauer et al, 2007).

The rational for using a range of industry sectors within the high tech sector as defined and discussed in chapter four is that many firms collaborate or form strategic alliances with firms outside their industry. Carrying out the research in this way will ensure that firms in their different development or life stages will be captured as well as those newer industries or firms.

1.6 Research objectives

The research question has evolved from the early literature review which highlights the fact that prior research undertaken in the areas of strategic management and particular the formulation and management of successful strategic alliances has focused on larger firms established for a number of years and are managed by management teams and not the owner manager. Therefore the study aims to enhance the body of knowledge through empirical research.

The study covers the relationships between individual managers and the influence that their demographics have on successful strategic alliances and individual firms and the success of the alliances.

It is well documented by policy makers that firms who are associated with regions where there is investment in infrastructures and local economy are likely to be successful. Researchers Chen and Karami (2010) have found that the perception of managers of SMEs is that location is not a critical success factor for them. Meanwhile there is a wealth of arguments about firms being situated on science or incubator parks Saffu and Mamman (1999) argue that there are many problems associated with such alliances including the different cultures. According to Elmuti et al (2005) There are benefits for both business and universities to working together and have highlighted some of these including knowledge and technology transfers on the other hand Kumaramanhalam (2005) suggests that it could be the profitability as an indicator of firm performance which is the bigger motivator for attracting investment. Furthermore it has to be asked is there a possibility of losing private alliances and funding if associated with academia.

1.7 Research question

How do management and firm demographics affect strategic alliance success in the high tech sector?

Research has been undertaken to ascertain the extent to which an individuals demographics influence their behaviour and decision making and affect firm performance (Goll et al, 2008). The interest of this study is how managers of SMEs individual demographics and characteristics influence their decision making, strategic management practices and their perceptions of the benefits of alliances. According to Dodourova (2009) success and failure factors are closely related to management perceptions which are formed from a range of managerial demographics and background characteristics such as age and experience. According to Goll et al (2008) a managers demographics including tenure and education are likely to have a positive effect on firm performance. Managers can exploit these capabilities to gain competitive advantage through strategic alliance formation.

The study is intended to reveal key demographics of managers and the firms themselves that might result in successful strategic alliances. As prior research has identified the need to create a profile of the respondents this will also be undertaken for this study. To do this a profile of both managers of small high tech firms and the firms themselves will be created to offer a robust definition of an owner manager of a small high tech firm operating in the turbulent environment of the high tech industry today. The profile of the manager will reveal characteristics that are common between the owners of SMEs in terms of age, education and strategic orientation. The profile of the firm will highlight demographics including firms in similar industries, size and level of technology.

To answer the research question the characteristics of both the manager and the studied firms will be identified together with their business strategy, to enable this research proposition one is presented below.

Proposition Identify key demographics of owner managers including gender, age, education and managerial experience to establish the affect that these demographics and background characteristics may have on alliance success. Identify key demographics of the studied firms to establish the relationship between firm's demographics and strategic alliance success.

Research Objective 1 To investigate the relationship between demographics and background characteristics of SME owners.

Hypothesis 1

H_1 There is significant Correlation between demographics and background characteristics of managers and strategic alliance success

Research Objective 2 To investigate the relationship between demographics and background characteristics of firms and strategic alliances.

Hypothesis 2

H_2 There is significant correlation between firms demographics and background characteristics and successful strategic alliances

1.8 Methodology

This is an empirical study undertaken in the high tech sector in the UK. The unit of analysis is the managers of the SMEs. Previous empirical research and the development of conceptual frameworks using managers as the unit of analysis has been successfully carried out (Berry, 1996; Jarratt, 1998; Kathuria and Porth, 2003; Shefer and Frenkel, 2005; Carmen et al, 2006; Dealtry, 2008; Chen and Karami, 2010; Haeussler et al, 2010).

Previously researchers have commented on the small sample numbers when targeting managers or CEOs, (Simsek et al, 2010) or who have chosen small samples due to the dispersed geography of their sample target (Jarratt, 1998).

The requirements of this study is to target a large sample, the best method to obtain this was to undertake a postal survey, a method found to have a high success in obtaining respondents (Chen and Karami, 2010) . This method is best used when the respondents are geographically dispersed and a large quantity of information needs to be obtained, it is also less costly and time consuming than interviews, case studies or group sessions. One of the main disadvantages of using a postal survey is that the variables have to be established in advance and the general construct of the target population has to be fairly well known. Due to the extensive literature on SMEs, generally the variables regarding manager's demographics and strategy are relatively easy to find, what was less easy was the variables relating to motivation on alliances.

Designing the questionnaire and conducting a pilot took some time, identifying questions and commonly used variables from prior research (Chen and Karami, 2010; Simsek et al, 2010) helped to construct a questionnaire that was likely to be completed.

Once questions that would enable testing of the hypothesis and answering the research questions were identified advice was taken from Hair et al (2007), Easterby-Smith et al (2008) and Saunders et al (2007) and construction of the questionnaire was underway using the following four principles;

1. Sequence the questions in descending order of importance and usefulness.

2. Group the questions that are similar in content or question type together.

3. Take advantage of the cognitive ties that respondents are likely to make among the groups of questions in deciding the order of the questions involved.

4. Position the questions that are more likely to be difficult after questions that are likely to be easier to answer.

The questionnaire was split into three sections enabling the respondent to see what the questions related to, it was hoped that this would elicit more consistent responses. Section one of the questionnaire required the managers to give demographic and background information about themselves, this information included gender, age, education level and managerial experience. Section two was designed to ask for demographic information about the firm, which included industry sector, age, size, and to identify the strategy employed by the firm.

Further questions asked for information about environmental scanning and managerial decision making, investment, R&D, sales, and the areas they might seek an alliance. Section three questions were related to the alliances themselves and included, engagement in alliances, responsibility for the alliance, how the company selects a partner, the technical success of the firm, and critical success factors of the alliance. The options for answering the questions were mostly tick boxes many with a simple choice of two options the remainder were measure on a five point Likert scale range from very important to not important.

The data collection involved sending out 5,000 questionnaires to the manager of SMEs in the high tech sector in the UK. The target respondents were thought to be most appropriate as they would not only be able to provide their own demographics but also the firms demographics and identify motivation and critical success factors for strategic alliance success. It was also considered appropriate as owner managers of SMEs would also be responsible for the type of strategy employed together with the use of any business tools to assist in managerial decision making.

On return the responses were coded and entered into SPSS for windows to enable data analysis to be carried out. Both descriptive and statistical analysis was undertaken. This included simple and cross tabulation, employment of Spearman Rank Order Correlation and the use of means and standard deviation to explore the data.

Once the data had been analysed and the hypothesis tested the results and findings were discussed. This involved synthesis the findings with incumbent literature and providing some explanation for the results. From the discussions some implications from the research for practitioners, policy makers and academics were identified.

1.9 Structure of the book

In order to achieve the research objectives through the pursuit of secondary and primary research this book will be structured to take the reader from the research proposal through to the research summary and conclusions. There are nine chapters in total each beginning with an introduction and ending with a summary or conclusion as appropriate.

The chapters are summarised in the following paragraphs. Where appropriate the chapters keep to the four themes i.e. management characteristics, firms characteristics, strategic alliance behaviour and strategic management. A profile is built of each of the key themes to assist with answering the research questions.

This chapter (chapter one) introduces the book topic, develops the research question and research objectives together with the research propositions and the hypothesis. The chapter outlines the background of the topic area including historical and contemporary issues regarding management theory in terms of strategic alliances. The rational for choosing this area to study is explained together with the aims and objectives of the research and the contribution to theory and knowledge.

Chapter two reviews the history of management to set the scene for management theory and practice today. The chapter seeks to highlight the plethora of theories around successful management with a view to highlighting the problems that firms may have if they are looking for tools or techniques to assist them as there is no one stop guide that will provide solutions for every business problem that a typical SME will encounter.

Chapter three presents the empirical literature review. The literature review is an essential part of the book as it provides background to the topic area and assists in identifying research questions posed and neglected by previous researchers.

In keeping with the four themes structure the body of the review will be carried out as follows.

- Firstly the main theoretical areas associated with strategic management are presented to inform the reader of the incumbent literature and its focuses and gaps.
- Secondly strategic alliance literature is reviewed.

- Thirdly synthesis of the literature to enable development of the conceptual framework.

Chapter four presents the conceptual framework. A strategic management model is adapted to view how managers in SMEs are expected to plan and facilitate their operations. Using literature key variables are identified to answer the research question. The four key themes are used to build a framework based on theoretical knowledge. Relationships are then suggested between management demographics, firm demographics and the management planning that results in firms' performance through successful strategic alliances.

Chapter five presents the methodology employed to conduct the research. There is a discussion on research paradigms, philosophies and design with rational for why certain approaches were adopted. The data collection methods are discussed together with a discussion on why the survey was considered a dependable method of data collection. The methods used for analysis are also discussed together with how reliability and validity of the research is measured. This chapter also presents the pilot study undertaken to enable proper development of the questionnaire.

Chapter six introduces the data analysis chapters which consist of chapters six and seven. The data analysis process presented in chapter five is discussed. Validation tests on the aggregated data are run to provide internal consistency. Descriptive statistics are employed to present the output from SPSS of the aggregated data using graphical and tabular formats to aid presentation.

Chapter seven presents the results from the statistical analysis that is undertaken to test the hypothesis, the results and findings of this chapter are presented and discussed in chapter eight.

Chapter eight presents the overall conclusions and discusses the findings of the research drawing on the descriptive and statistical analysis presented in chapters six and seven. The main themes of the study are revisited and interpretation of the results are reported.

Chapter nine concludes the book with a report of the major findings and presents the major findings. Recommendations for future research are given after considering the limitations of this study and the findings. Guidelines for practitioners are provided based on the literature and the best practices reported by the managers during the survey. Contributions to the knowledge and policy implications are also discussed

Chapter Two: Theoretical background to the study

2.1 Introduction

The main theory that underpins this research is strategic management. It is recognised that strategic management is how managers evaluate, plan and execute their long term goals. This chapter is split into three sections. Section one reviews the theoretical background to management theory presenting a time line of the theories as they evolved. Section two covers analysis of the high tech sector in the UK. Section three defines alliance types. Each section begins with an introduction and ends in a summary for that section.

2.2 Management Theory

As management studies have increased over the decades so have theories evolved. Schools of management thought have evolved building framework which continue to have an impact on current managerial behaviour and decision making. Meanwhile management planning, strategic management and strategies have all been lumped together to explain how management decision making can impact on firm performance (Harrison and Taylor, 1996; Covin and Slevin, 1998; Barringer and Bluedorn, 1999; Atuahene-Gima and Ko, 2001; Cui and Mak, 2002; Stonehouse and Pemberton, 2002; Alvesson and Sveningsson, 2003; Analoui and Karami, 2003; Stewart et al, 2003; During et al, 2005; Day et al, 2006; Grinstein and Goldman, 2006; Dobbs and Hamilton,

2007; Jackson, 2007; Adcroft and Willis, 2008; French, 2009; Chou and Yang, 2011) as they discuss management in all its dimensions. The danger of this is that it is not clear what is the influencer and what is the influenced and paradoxical paradigms do not help in understanding the complexity of management decision making and the instigation of strategic management.

Each of the key areas of management will be discussed throughout the study however those which cause issues are through rhetoric are unravelled here to reduce ambiguity or confusion elsewhere. To provide a contextual background to this study these themes are briefly discussed to explain the importance of key factors such as strategic management in contributing to firm performance. Strategic management (Jauch and Glueck, 1988; Morden, 2007) comes about through management scanning their environments and making decisions, (Hough and White, 2004) a simple definition made more complicated by the irrationality of man and environments that do not remain stable. This necessitates a whole discourse on what ifs, impacters, influencers, the influenced and can only be explained away by the careful considerations of manager's previous experiences and how they learn from the experiences of each other.

2.2.1 History of management theory

As briefly introduced in chapter one modern organisations evolved during the middle of the nineteenth century when mass automated production was introduced. Management thinking did not evolve at the same pace as the technology. The classical school of management was preceded by the pre classicists however these did not introduce the management systems we are familiar with today instead one concentrated on improving human resources and the other looked at ways of increasing profit. They did however pave the way for the father of the classical school and in particular bureaucratic management Max Weber. Weber set in motion the idea that hierarchies were necessary to ensure that those at the top had control and power. F W Taylor and Frank and Lillian Gilbreth founders of the scientific management again concentrated on management and in particular ways of increasing productivity Mousa and Lemak (2009. Taylor's premise that employees should be closely supervised goes against the way we consider close supervision as having negative impact on the employee and therefore the firm.

Pryor and Taneja (2010) review the influence of Henry Fayol whose management practices are still widely used in organisations today was an advocate for administration which was another branch of the classical school of management. Management theory and practice continued to develop and the work of Mary Follett closely followed by Elton Mayos Hawthorn experiments explained away behaviour of employees and gave birth to behaviour management. The Hawthorne experiment uncovered the fact that workers are not motivated by money past a point and the result was the advent of the human relations movement. The most influential researchers at this time were Maslow and McGregor (Bassett-Jones and Lloyd, 2005: Weisbord, 2011). These were followed by Likert, Herzberg and McClelland, increasingly these worked on improving management decision making and striving to improving working conditions. They examined further those ideas started by Mayo into motivation and needs of employees (Bassett-Jones and Lloyd, 2005).

This brings us to contemporary management theories and begins to focus more on the actions of managers and the need to be focused on organisational management, the work of Deming and Drucker are most influential in this contemporary school of management.

As well as these schools of thought over the decades other theories and management paradigms have been presented and today the systems approach and contingency approach are used in many organisations the latter is focused on the experience and judgements of the manager to control the organisation by focusing on the environment.

2.2.2 What is strategy?

It has been discussed that, "Strategy is the direction and scope of an organization over the long term which achieves advantage in a changing environment through its configuration of resources and competences with the aim of fulfilling stakeholder expectations"(Johnson et al, 2008, p3) confirming the findings of Byars (1987). The term strategy has also been defined as "the means by which the enterprise achieves its objectives" (Morden, 2007, p184).

A question raised by (Porter, 1996) which he explains fully according to his own research and widely used models, however, other writers have their own definitions and may relate to the era in which they were writing or the approach they favour (Mintzberg, 1987). Historical definitions of strategy has focused on their need for careful planning more recent writers such as (Hill and Jones

1989; Mintzberg et al, 1998) put forward a good argument that strategies do not just come from careful planning but emerge due to changes in the external and internal environment. Recent corroboration for this comes from (Pillania, 2009). Through the process of strategic management in decision making and implementing the strategies, advantages can be gained for organizations in both markets and stakeholder expectations (Beverland and Bretherton, 2001).

According to Pillania (2009) strategy is still a concept that is subject to interpretation and he points out that the use, formulation and implementation is down to individual managers. It is also implied in the literature that when a company maintains it has a strategy expectations are held that there is a plan available which is infallible and if followed success is assured.

Research shows that there is evidence in the records of strategic planning businesses that they expand more often than those who use strategic or financial control (Goold and Cambell, 1987), this is corroborated by Porter (1996). Mintzberg, (1987) argues that strategy is a consideration of the past experiences and future opportunities resulting in planning a factor all businesses have to consider and those that do not generally fail.

2.2.3 What is strategic management?

Strategic Management (sm) terminology is not easily defined in the literature as authors use words interchangeably leaving it open to interpretation and perception (Byers, 1987; Jauch, 1988; Mintzberg et al, 1998; Hill and Jones, 1989; Porter, 1996). It even goes as far as to deliberately mislead (Byast and Karami, 2009; French, 2009) leading to a failure to distinguish between the concepts of strategic management, strategy and planning (Stonehouse and Pemberton, 2002; Byast and Karami, 2009). As a result of these finding the words will continue to be used interchangeably through the study although it is understood that to formulate and implement strategies or plans management decisions must be made.

Literature focusing on SMEs, sm or type of strategy as defined above has not differentiated between service and industrial businesses, and in most instances the research has been conducted in one industry or country so it is not clear if it could be applied to other countries or sectors who each have their own individual problems, competition and restrictions due to political climates. (French, 2004; Kraus et al, 2006; Pasanen and Laukkanen, 2006; Singh et al, 2006; Dobbs and Hamilton, 2007; Glaister et al, 2008; Johnston et al, 2008; Meeham and Lindsey, 2008; Moriarty and Jones, 2008; O'Regan et al, 2008; Byast and Karami, 2009).

The recent chronology of these works indicates that the increase in the number of SMEs and their role in the economy has generated an interest in them. They are now seen as a separate species having a set of particular needs. These needs must be addressed to fulfil goals, aims and objectives. The route to achieving their goals may not be the same strategy frameworks employed by larger firms (Fiet, 2008).

Reviewing the authors who have defined this question has resulted in as many answers as there are authors as this subject is in early stages of development compared to other business theories Stonehouse and Pemberton (2002) and as discussed earlier terminology and concept is not clearly defined. A problem with SM is that factors can change before the strategy has been fully implemented. Mintzberg (1987) proposes that it is difficult to decide a long term plan and that strategies which emerge over time is the best way for modern companies. Again this may be more to do with individual mangers or individual sectors and whether they lead or impose and who has been involved in the decision making (Mullins, 2005). Furthermore early empirical evidence in the incumbent literature suggests that SMEs do not engage in formal planning as per the models in existence.

The majority of these models are created with concepts derived from those associated with larger firms and which do not transform successfully to SMEs. Further evidence suggests that SMEs rarely engage in formal planning and that the managers perceive the benefits of strategic management as being minimal and not having a big impact on performance. Despite this there is limited evidence that strategic management drawn from successful environmental and market scanning does result in firm performance which is superior to that of firms who employ neither.

2.2.4 Benefits of strategic management

The development of management decision making evolved into this phenomena of strategic management partly due to the rise in numbers of small competing firms. As environmental turbulence increased these firms looked for ways to control their environments and one way was to carry out extensive environmental analysis with a view to understanding the competition, markets and the shortening of life cycles as innovative products invaded the market demanded by increasingly sophisticated consumers who had more disposable income to purchase these products or the access to credit for the same. Managers felt the need to develop pro active stances rather than rely on reactive measures with which to manage their businesses.

Mintzberg argues that strategies need to be emergent to allow for flexibility Porter asserts that every firm competing within an industrial sector must have a competitive strategy whether this has been devised through a formal planning process or has evolved through the coordination of various functions.

There are a number of reasons that formal strategic management is not appropriate for SMEs in the high tech sector and there is little empirical evidence to significantly support the assertion that firms without formal strategic management are less successful than formal planners.

Firms measure success in different ways, efficient managers who thoroughly understand their firm and the market may not be considered strategic managers but may still be successful. A formal planning system which is poorly constructed or employed may be more detrimental than not having a plan.

SMEs environments change so fast they may not be able to be flexible if constrained by bureaucracy and formal plans that can not be changed. As discussed in chapter one managers are irrational and subjected to issues throughout the business life cycle while theories suggest rationalised decision making

As can be seen there are some risks to formalising strategy so that it becomes a mantra for the firm and is not used to measure managerial performance. Strategic management is seen as an add on to day to day management which can cause problems and in the interest of this study in particular when strategic alliances are considered as a solution to a crisis and not part of the strategic management of the firm.

Through literature review a definition of strategy and strategic management is proposed

"Strategic management is the actions of a manager when formulating a plan, implementing it and evaluating the outcomes and objectives achieved following a period of intense environmental analysis resulting in management decision making".

Therefore I proposes that in addition

"strategic management is the process of analysis, decision and action resulting in the achievement of a firms increased performance".

2.2.5 The process and value of carrying out strategic management research

It is widely acknowledge that management requires the development of integrated frame works to support management decision making. However there is still some disharmony in the way it is carried out Byars (1987) suggests there are two stages to SM decision making and implementation while Jauch (1988) suggests that it is usually carried out as three separate functions; choice, implementation, and evaluation.

Empirical research shows that there is a correlation between strategic planning and organizational performance and results show that long term planning does increase performance (Kraus et al, 2006). A main indicator for growth was employment growth this is a good indicator of real growth as profit may be high in other studies however if the money is not being used to grow the business this may not be a good indicator of performance (Collier, 2006). This is corroborated by (Pasanen and Laukkanen, 2006) who argue that firm performance is a core issue in strategic management. Businesses involved in Strategic Management are generally more aware of changes in external environments and can act accordingly (O'Regan et al, 2008) however it is generally agreed that micro firms are more flexible than larger ones even in turbulent environments (Mason, 2007).

There is evidence that the debate about characteristics of strategy and its place in the processes of SMEs is ongoing and this specifically applies to Strategic Management and strategic decision making. There are a number of areas however where the agenda is quite clear.

2.2.6 Management decision making

Managers of SMEs are clearly the developers of strategic management as they are the ones with the overarching view of the firm and are able to view the organisation holistically and consider integrations of its processes. This is further supported in SME studies where the owner is often the manager and therefore has full control strategic or otherwise of the firm.

There is an implication of resource distribution when making strategic decisions as strategic management involves multi functional issues and managers must decide were to invest their resources, time or otherwise.

Decision making has a long term impact on the firm and its performance. It also has an impact on long term relationships with external stakeholders such as customers, suppliers, competitors and these may be in the terms of something more formal such as alliances or forward or backward integration. Strategic management and its inherent process is more complex than other aspects of business management and is partly due to;

• Managers make decisions in periods of uncertainty

• Managers look at trends to gauge future competition

• Decision making is based on guesswork as often facts are not available.

- Managers have difficulty in combining priorities of different functions.

As a result of the above any decisions made and strategy formed with a view to strategic management will impact throughout the lifecycle of the business and during each process.

Decision making which results in strategy formulation usually occurs after an organisation has identified that a change, improvement, or diversification is needed. Singh et al, (2008) confirm findings that to date SMEs have not been noted for developing effective strategies nor benchmarking (Thakkar et al, 2008) themselves against trends as argued by (Dobbs and Hamilton, 2007) this is not an effective way to ascertain their future potential for growth.

2.2.7 Decision makers

Who will be responsible for the decision making? Managers of SMEs are often used to making the decisions themselves and may find it difficult to share the responsibility or delegate it to some one else. Problems may arise and this may depend on the formality of the alliance, the hierarchy of control and the expected outcomes. Managers who are used to making the decisions may resent contributions from other managers and therefore this needs to be clear from the outset. There may be turbulent emotions around sharing. Trust and motivation for engagement in the first place.

2.2.8 Frequency of strategic management application in SMEs

Evidence (Johnson et al, 2008; Chell, 2001) has shown that large corporations employ Strategic Management and these feature regularly as case studies for success, however, research in the less explored area of SME and Strategic Management or indeed the use of strategy does not show the same usage of these useful tools and techniques to ensure growth and differentiation between themselves and the competition (Porter 1996).

Researched based evidence shows that a high number of SMEs do have a business plan (Karami, 2007) however this did not mean that they had long-range plans or that they were inflexible and the more detailed analysis separated those that had mission statements and had carried out robust environmental scanning prior to formulating their plans. While this research is extensive and analysed using many variables it, like previous literature has a focus (although not deliberately) on heavy industry and does not explore service sector or micro businesses. The results could be an indication that production and manufacturing need planning to enable control of resources, marketing and distribution while some high tech industries are flexible due to the often intangible nature of their offerings. It is the view while undertaking this study that whether managers are formal or informal planners they must plan otherwise they will plan to fail.

2.2.9 Effectiveness of strategic management in SMEs

Research indicates that SME managers are more likely to focus on day to day functions such as finance for survival rather than the growth process Singh et al, (2008) although their research is based on review rather than empirical findings, their views are corroborated by Stonehouse and Pemberton, (2002) whose key findings indicate that managers do not find strategic management essential to their planning process. Through this study it is hoped that empirical findings will show that as firms mature then they do become more strategic and build in strategies rather than crisis manage.

SMEs are poor at developing strategies. Rather they are more intent on survival (Singh et al, 2008; Kumar and Antony, 2008) present findings about the lack of quality management practices suggesting a number of reasons for this including resources and lack of knowledge. If this is true then it is expected that Managers in the high tech sectors will engage in alliances to increase their knowledge and will look for complementary collaborators.

2.2.10 What is strategic planning?

It is emphasised throughout literature that strategic planning benefits the firm by coordinating activities to reach long term goals. Integrated frameworks are developed to support management decision making. This is an indication that managers realise that to survive in unstable environments they need to develop a management style which would be flexible to cope with these changes but static enough to use its existing resources and competencies to be competitive.

According to Ansoff (1991) and Jauch, (1988) it is the managers ability to develop strategies for the firm, engage in new organisational capabilities and guide the firm towards a new strategic position and it is the successful integration of these three that suggest the manager is engaging in strategic management. Strategic management is the process of making decisions and taking action to implement those decisions to ensure survival and growth of the business. Further more Goold and Cambell, (1987) identified three successful styles of managing strategy and emphasized that there could not be one best way and that there would always be a factor of "it depends".

2.2.11 Growth strategies in SMEs

There is little evidence of literature focusing directly on growth strategies in SMEs rather the focus is on individual functions such as marketing or finance Reynolds and Lancaster, (2007). It is also unremarkable that this literature has been published in the last five years highlighting the swing from industrial to service sector and large organizations to SMEs. Strategy formulation and the relevance in SMEs is a key feature of modern literature (Analoui and Karami, 2003; Karami, 2007; Singh et al, 2008) together with the importance of understanding the environment in which they operate however there is still a dearth of research around the types of strategies, models and frameworks adopted.

2.2.12 Environmental analysis in micro businesses

According to Garengo et al (2005) and Garengo and Bititci (2007) it is assumed that environmental changes affect all businesses. Considering the wealth of literature dedicated to the external factors on a business it is clearly a matter for investigating. This research has investigated the importance of the trends which are currently affecting businesses and these include political trends such as decreases in taxation, economic factors in particular light of the reduced interests rates and the fact that banks are not lending to businesses. Businesses are also affected by rivals, suppliers, buyers and these are also investigated in this section.

2.2.13 The importance of the external environmental factors

As discussed in the literature review, the use of strategic management assumes the creation and implementation of business strategies. It is important therefore that the critical factors that could affect a business are considered when creating strategies. While internal factor analysis of the organization are important strengths, weaknesses, threats and opportunities (SWOT) the external factors are equally if not more important considerations as business owners have little or no control over them.

44

2.2.14 Issues for alliance management

In literature there has been a focus on the failure of alliances with little evidence of how these firms are being assisted to diminish the risk of failure. Through this study it is anticipated that by learning from other managers experience and how they perceive alliances a model will be constructed which will enable firms who employ it or similar methods to be more confident about engaging and managing their alliances.

According to Lorange and Roos (1992 pp 124) "The size and complexity of the strategic alliance also plays a role regarding the relative emphasis on formal planning and control". Therefore it can be seen that managers need to have a balance between the amount of control it has on the activities of the alliance with the need to build a relationship with the partner which may take the firms working together beyond this particular alliance and may do this even if the alliance fails for reasons other than non compliance or firm incompatibility. There are areas of alliances where paradoxes occur, competition and co-operations and these will need to be overcome before they develop into conflicts or problems between partners.

2.2.15 Technological advancement

As discussed in chapter one management systems have not developed as quickly as technology. This phenomena has been researched in detail by others who consider the way management of this technology has occurred and how this has contributed to expansion of the sector of high tech firms.

2.3 SMEs in the high tech sector in the UK

This section reviews the high tech sector in the UK as a preamble to the study. The sector is reviewed with an exploration of incumbent firms and their contribution to the economy.

Despite lagging behind in some industries the UK high tech sector have become more proactive and is acknowledge as being leaders in research and development (OECD, 2010) This has been assisted by the government's policy of investment in science, technology and incubator parks which specialize in supporting organic R&D businesses in a range of scientific and technology areas.

Auditing these firms has proved problematic due to the lack of heterogeneity and it is not possible to estimate correctly the number of small high tech firms in the UK as data is counted and held by different bodies and there is a lack of an established database of SMEs in the high tech firms in the UK (Jones-Evans and Westhead,

1996). The most up to date figures are reported by the Annual Business Inquiry (2008).

"there are approximately 132,000 establishments in the Semta

footprint in the UK, employing just over 1.7 million people"

Source Semta (2010)

According to Jones-Evans and Westhead (1996 pp 16) the increase in small high technology firms came from what they call the "flexible specialization theory" explaining the phenomena of high tech high growth firms development during recession periods as being an interaction of "demand side, supply side and policy factors".

Firms whose processes or products require a high degree of scientific or technological knowledge are often grouped as high tech firms (Rhyne et al, 1997). They usually invest in R&D and employ technically qualified personnel. Therefore these two measures are used for identifying small high tech firms for the purpose of this study.

Firms who chose to compete in this area face rapid changes and short product life cycles and the OECD (2010) gives classification of the high tech sector to include the following industries which have been adopted globally;

2.3.1 High-tech sectors

Currently the majority of high tech firms come under the higher level classification of manufacturing activities. The OECD definition of manufacturing is;

"the physical and or chemical transformation of materials, substances or components into new products".

The material substances or components are raw materials which are products of agriculture, forestry, fishing or mining as well as products and semi-finished products of other manufacturing activities. with new divisions introduced to represent important new industries or old industries which may have increased their economic or social relevance. Division 21 for the manufacture of basic pharmaceutical products and division 26 for the manufacture of computer, electronic and optical products while the manufacture of computers is presented in division 30 (ONS stats 2007). Further classifications comes from the OECD who measure research intensity and the usage rate of technology into account under their broader manufacturing classifications.

This sector approach of classifying industries according to their technology intensity, product approach and according to finished products implies that high tech firms can be found in and within sectors. Using SIC codes identified broad areas of sectors and therefore firms who responded may be in a sector but do not consider themselves to be high tech they may only be contracting to larger firms or using technology as a component of their own product. The classifications from different sources also yield different results while new technology such as that used in gaming and remote computerised assistance and call centres is not adequately described in the definitions of high tech firms. Other sectors containing firms such as information technology development are not necessarily considered high tech however, they may be considered as high tech due to the use of information technology development by other firms.

Broad categories of sectors are presented below;

- Aerospace technology
- Artificial intelligence
- Biotechnology
- Chemical
- Energy
- Instrumentation
- Nanotechnology
- Nuclear Physics
- Optoelectronics
- Robotics
- Telecommunications
- Electrical Engineering

In 2008 Hellebrandt and Davies carried out research into the classification of industries within the manufacturing sector. They examine the methodology used to place enterprises within an area of economic activity and view how the results can be misleading in terms of calculating numbers employed within a sector and indeed how many firms reside in each sector. They hypothesise some of the reasons that firms categorisation can change over time one of the problems encountered in this study when firms cannot be easily counted nor categorised.

The high tech sector is synonymous with innovation. Innovation is important to the growth of an economy, and successful innovation requires a balance between demand and supply. In today's knowledge economy, intangible assets such as skills and knowledge are increasingly important. Innovation is no longer seen purely as a product of scientific research and development, instead, it can come from changes in processes or procedures that can be driven by consumers in their quest for more personalised products and services (Nesta, 2010).

Innovation is at the centre of UK policy to close the productivity gap. Innovation is the 'successful exploitation of new ideas'. To ensure ideas are successful, a proposition must be viable.

EIPR's definition encompasses some of the wider typologies; "Innovation is about change and the ability to manage change over time. Innovation can be about the successful exploitation of new ideas in the form of a new or improved product or service but it can also be about the way in which a product or service is delivered. Equally, innovation can be about creatively positioning (or marketing) an existing product, or about changing the business model (a new 'paradigm', such as low-cost airlines)." Criteria for success can include market share, number of sales, profit made, diffusion rate, beating competitors, or changes in user behaviour. There are various typologies of innovation, but in general they cover three categories:

- Product innovation (new goods and services).

- Process innovation (new technologies and techniques to adjust production or delivery).
-
- Organisational innovation (new ways to organise work practices and business models).

Within each type of innovation there are three levels of innovation:

- Incremental – small continuous improvements that cause relatively little disruption, e.g. a new invoicing system.
- Radical – new to the market or firm, often disruptive to the industry, discontinuous, e.g. a new product for sale or a new business model such as home delivery for a retailer.
- Transformational – new to the world, rare but big innovations that cut across all industries, e.g. the World Wide Web.

High-tech exports have usually been used as an indicator of the capacity of a country to exploit R&D outcomes and transform them into advanced goods to be sold on global markets. However, as globalisation becomes a door open to more and the advent of countries such as China as a big exporter of high-tech products means that using high-tech exports as an indicator of a knowledge-based economy becomes less straightforward. This section also analyses other indicators of knowledge-intensity in the economy, such as value added and employment type in the high tech sector.

As agreed by OECD (2010; Berr and Nesta 2010; 2011, IDBR and Europa the high tech industries are a source of economic growth for the UK. There is a focus on these firms being innovative and efficient in research and development (R&D).

There are a number of private, government sponsored, and education sponsored researchers in to the policies, behaviour and future of SMEs in the high tech sector. Despite this wealth of information it also causes some problems due to ambiguity in the measurement of the data between organisations with the UK often being cited as part of the EU 27. This may lead to some disparity in the figures presented in this section as they are often compiled from multiple sources however there is uniformity in the assertion that SMEs in the high tech sector contribute to the economy.

The data used for illustration purposes in this section comes from a number of sources and has been aggregated in some cases to obtain figures for the UK. The standard industrial classification (SIC) codes from 2003 have been used to identify high tech firms as a significant portion of the data was obtained pre 2007 when SIC codes were changed to account for new industrial sectors within existing categories. These sectors include those that are in the manufacturing sector and research and development categories but does not include consultancy, B2B suppliers or computer repair firms.

Furthermore, OECD's product-based classification supports the technology intensity approach. It can be concluded that companies in a high-technology industry do not necessary produce high-technology products and vice versa. This further creates a problem of aggregation.

2.3.2 New firms

Data on firm birth and death rates is limited in scope and subject to variations because of different recording methods however research has recorded the increase in SMEs in the high tech sector and also the high rate of failures, despite which entrepreneurs continue to invest time and money into new projects. Figure 2.1 illustrates the percentage of SMEs by size in each of the sectors.

High tech SMES have been cited as accounting for a significant portion of revenue from all high tech industries. In 2006 SMEs contributed over 60% of total revenue from all the high tech industries. These figures from ONS (2010) may differ from those supplied from eurostat or OECD due to the reporting periods and classifications used, also those included in the definition of SME can vary, also figures are often subjected to seasonal adjustments.

Many of the UK firms have the benefit of having portfolio of products or brands which means they are continually able to input into their research and development. Reid and Garnsey (1997) note that despite considerable attention given to the activity of innovation there is little evidence about the survival and performance of these firms in terms of their involvement with technology or science parks. When firms graduate from incubation of science parks they often do so as a consequence of acquisition and mergers or failure.

Despite the number and importance of new and small firms, there has been little explicit examination of their strategies. Founders of new firms must find ways to compete in a world which had gotten along without them before. Starting with no reputation and limited financial and human resources, they must seek out opportunities and develop strategies which enable them to compete, sometimes in industries dominated by larger, established companies. Since almost any strategy involves competing with someone, they need to consider which established competitors might be challenged and whether sustainable competitive advantages could be achieved (Cooper et al, 1986).

Figure 2.1   High Tech Firms by size and sector

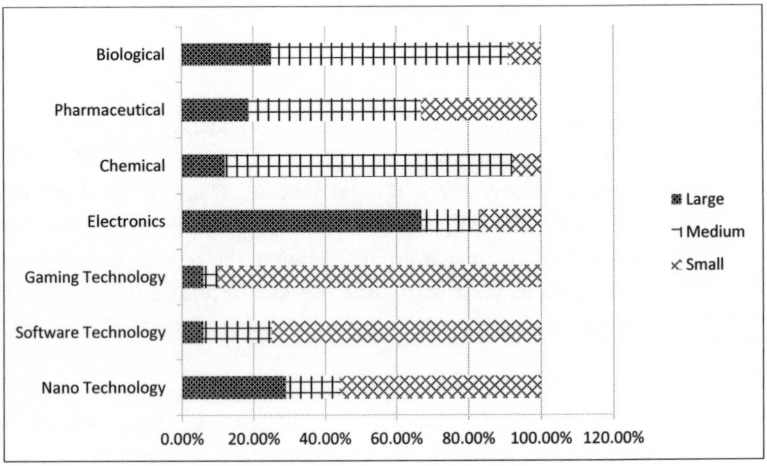

Source ONS (2007)

2.4. Alliance formation in the high tech sector in the UK

A number of studies have indicated that successful collaborations occur in the larger firms. There is an increasing body of work that suggests that while small firms prefer to look inward for their investments, resources and capabilities many recognise the value of cooperation (Ireland et al, 2002; Oxley and Sampson, 2004; Chin et al, 2008; Chen and Karami, 2010; Das and Kumar, 2010).

There are a range of alliance types currently being exploited and these are discussed more fully in chapter four but cover the wide areas of joint venture, strategic alliances, sub-contracting and licensing.

Despite the abundance of alliance formation in high tech SMEs they are still doomed to failure and while tackling resource constraints to bring their products to market there are still factors which prevent these innovative firms from successful alliances. The literature for example Hagedoorn (2002) has focused on alliances between large companies and little research has focused on the motivations for smaller firms to form alliances. Figure 2.2 illustrates recent partner preferences for SMEs in the high tech sector.

Figure 2.2 Partnership formation by partner type

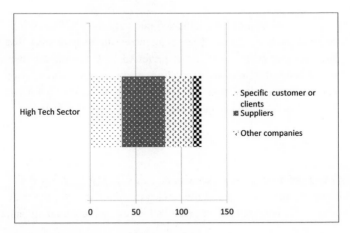

Source; European Commission (2009);

As SMEs face disadvantages when exploiting their technologies it would be a justified assumption that they would be motivated to engage in alliances.

As data is scarce or not readily available in a useable format data from all sources available have been used. This enables illustration of the rise in strategic alliances, investment, number of high tech firms over the past decades. The following data and figures have been sourced from Hagedoorn (2002). Figure 2.3 demonstrates the decline in joint ventures over the last three decades however more recent research indicates a rise in strategic alliances as an option over other forms of cooperation.

Figure 2.3 The share (%) of joint ventures in all newly established R&D partnerships (1960–1998)

Source Hagedoorn (2002)

The data in figure 2.4 is over three decades old however it demonstrates and corroborates contemporary research that pharmaceutical firms are proactive in engaging in partnerships.

Figure 2.4   Relative contractual partnering indexes, per sector (1960-1998)

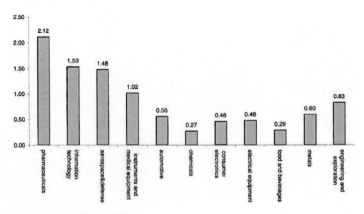

Source Hagedoorn (2002)

According to Berry (1996) while investment in basic research is a prerequisite for technological change and economic efficiency Pavitt (1993) suggests that such an emphasis leads to the assumption that scientific invention inevitably results in technological innovation, which in turn creates economic competitiveness (Newby, 1993). A major shortcoming of this approach is that the development of new technology does not in itself guarantee commercial success for firms operating in domestic and international markets. Many other management factors will play a significant part in determining the viability of the business and the firm's achievements in the long term.

The presence of a diversified management team, in which technological expertise is balanced with business skills in other areas such as marketing and finance, is recognized as a determinant of success in technology-based start-ups (Roberts, 1968; Cooper, 1973; Segal Quince and Partners, 1985; Smith and Fleck, 1987). Similarly, previous studies have highlighted that strategy formulation and the leadership qualities of key managers are critical success factors in relation to the evolution of innovative small high-tech firms (Dodgson and Rothwell, 1991; Curran et al, 2009; Chen and Karami, 2010).

2.4.1 Inter firm partnerships

This section of chapter two analyses different forms of inter-firm agreements and explains classifications and definitions.

Alliances and in particular strategic ones are a fairly new organisational structure compared to other types of organisational structure in the High Tech Industries. Previous research has not cleared the confusion about what an alliance is when compared to a merger or acquisition especially as many failed alliances have resulted in a takeover either hostile or friendly.

2.4.2 Why is definition necessary?

Historically researchers have used strategic alliances to describe any type of partnership which is formed between at least two companies.

Soosay et al (2008) notes that upstream/downstream integrated relationships are also often called strategic alliances or collaborations.

Lorange and Roos (1993) use terms interchangeable as do others when presenting joint ventures, consortiums and licensing agreements as strategic alliances.

As one of the research focuses is on the engagement with strategic alliances in the high tech Industry it is necessary to compare strategic alliances with other types of agreements to better understand their importance.

In 2002 the Harvard Business Review (2002) published a special edition dedicated to the topic of strategic alliances testament to their importance in the modern economy.

Historically alliances have been classed as hybrid organisational structures (Williamsons, 1985; Lin and Lin, 2010) or inter-organisational relationships (Lin and Darling, 1999) networks (Gomes-Casseres, 2002) collaborative business arrangements (Soosay et al, 2008)

Within these groups there is a spectrum of mergers and acquisitions, formal and informal agreements etc. This section continues with a description of these alliance types using where possible evidence of their dominance in the High Tech SMEs.

2.4.3 Mergers and acquisitions

Many companies formulate strategies that take the offensive (Clarke Hill et al, 2003) when this is done predatory firms circle and acquisitions occur. A powerful or experienced company buys out a weaker company to obtain its resources and skills but not always keeping the firms identity (Anslinger and Copeland, 1998). These differ slightly from mergers which are less offensive and are a result of two firms combining together to form a new company. These two forms are used interchangeably in literature. The Thatcher regime which bought about deregulation made these popular as incumbent firms needed to strengthen their competitive advantage when confronted by new competition.

2.4.4 Joint ventures

Joint ventures occur when two independent companies come together and form a third stand-alone company, often with the purpose of performing a specific task. Both the parent companies may have some input into the company and receive some of the outputs, however the company is run independently. Joint ventures are usually formed to exploit new market opportunities, share costs and risks or to gain local knowledge (Nanda and Williamson, 2002). Despite the diverse range of research on Joint Ventures in the High Tech little has focused on their success or reasons for entering into this type of partnership.

Many of the Joint Ventures in the High Tech Industry are only for one part of the process or operations this allows companies to enjoy economies of scale and scope while protecting their intellectual property.

2.4.4.1 Strategic alliances

Co-operation between firms whether formal or informal are known as strategic alliances (SA) (Lin and Darling, 1999). Formal alliances are held by legal agreements while informal tend to be a verbal agreement, thereby necessitating the need for mutual trust between the partners (Hughes and Beasley, 2008).

Unlike Joint Ventures and Mergers and Acquisitions both firms keep corporate identities and most will have safe guards in place to retain their culture, skills and resources (except those that are required to form the Strategic Alliance. It can be seen that a new organisation does not occur rather it is a partnership where each firm has roles and responsibilities held together by mutual drivers, motivation and trust brought together by skilful negotiation. As the term Strategic Alliance is used the implication is that it is planned with a long term view.

A Strategic Alliance provides the companies with new capabilities often without purchases, the benefits of which are more than financial gains indeed (Hagedoorn and Schakenraad, 1994: Saffu and Mamman, 1999) purport that quick financial expectations can lead to the early termination of a SA. Mutual need and trust is meant to hold the relationship together (Hughes and Beasley, 2008).

2.4.4.2 Classification of alliances

Alliances are classified according to how integrated they are. Research suggests that most fall into the category of formal and informal co- operative ventures. There is little evidence of mergers and acquisitions between SMEs while literature is abundant with those in MNEs. However SMEs still remain prey to predatory companies who are looking for firms to add to their portfolios.

Mergers and acquisitions totally integrate firms so are at one end of the spectrum while joint ventures which are only integrated to form specific tasks are nearer the middle. Informal ventures who only share between departments is nearer the other end of the spectrum.

The error in these classifications is that each partner has the same attached importance to the degree of integration and interdependence. However as discussed by (Lorange and Roos, 1993; Lin and Darling, 1999) each partner will have differing perspectives on the alliance. For this reason they propose an alternative based on how much each partner will invest and take from the alliance.

A decision will need to be made on whether the investment is long or short term and will decide if the outputs generated by the alliance will be reinvested into the alliance for future projects or shared between the partners.

A problem with many of the solutions is that they are all variations on the theme of joint ventures often used by companies as an alternative to altering their internal structures when environmental turbulence occurs (Nanda and Williamson, 2002)

2.4.4.3 Pooling

Pooling occurs when only one partner operates but both share in the cost and risks of the venture. This may occur in the form of business angels or other investor involvement. The advantage of this is the avoidance of predatory firms taking over. Weaker firms are guaranteed survival. There is however, a danger that partners will withdraw if predicted profits are not realised.

2.4.4.4 Strategic or tactical alliances

Strategic alliances (SA) allows for cooperation in a wide range of activities from sales, marketing purchasing, maintenance and because they are formed to give the partners a competitive edge over their competition and benefits are seen to be long term. On the other hand tactical alliances focus on only one area and are often designed to reap short term benefits.

2.5 Chapter summary

This chapter has introduced the main areas of concern for this study i.e. management, SMEs and alliances within the high tech sector. Each of the main areas have been reviewed from a historical viewpoint using literature and government statistics and documents to aid classification of firms and industries.

Changes in the environment and conditions under which managers have to function suggest that a new paradigm for researching them is necessary no longer can we assume that they can be grouped together and treated as being the same it is necessary to understand the paradoxes that surround SMEs and to treat them accordingly. Seeking out new models by which they can assess their abilities and firm capabilities while scanning the environment are being created and in chapter four a new model for considering management and strategic alliances for SMEs is presented.

It is implied through literature that those firms who employ strategic management are performing better than those who do not and in terms of this study the strategic behaviour of the managers will be considered when measuring their successful alliances.

Due to the shortened life cycle of technology based products in an ever competing market it can be seen that having a strategy and long term goals would be beneficial to SMEs and that technology, market and customers must be aligned in the strategy.

This section has reviewed the small high tech sector in the UK to explain the contribution to the economy. The government and other bodies have invested significant amounts of money into the high tech sector in the UK particularly into the research and development stage. Despite this high costs associated with new innovations make it difficult for SMEs to patent and register their products and thereby protecting their intellectual property which leaves them fair game to predatory larger firms.

Chapter Three: Literature Review

3.1 Introduction

A literature review is "secondary analysis of explicit knowledge". It is usually carried out using library physical or electronic resources. This is usually concluded with a written appraisal of the literature and if necessary the identification of limitations or gaps in the literature. The literature review therefore provides a historical overview of theory, concepts and abstracts of the research area under consideration.

3.2 Literature review strategy

Within research there are two main literature review strategies one follows the traditional review method which concerns reading and critically writing about what is known about a topic and the other is systematic which follows a prescribed methodology with 6 stages as defined by Jesson et al (2011) as follows;

Define the research question

Design the plan

Search for literature

Apply exclusion and inclusion criteria

Apply quality assessment

Synthesise

For the purpose of this book a traditional review of the literature has been undertaken, however some of the rigours of the systematic review have been employed to ensure validity of the journals reviewed.

3.2.1 Obtaining the literature

The University's e-resources database was initially used to identify prominent publishers of literature pertaining to management, strategic management, strategic alliances, marketing and firm performance. A large number of publishers were returned initially which included Emerald, Wiley Black, Science Direct. Initially choosing the Emerald database and inserting key words in the e-resource database search engine such as strategy, strategic alliances, SMEs, R&D, high tech firms and innovation showed over 140,000 articles, journals and full text on the subject of strategic alliances and related topics requiring the need for a primed search query which would result in a comprehensive bibliography following some modification to the search. A further selection process took place using the bibliographies of a number of the most relevant journal articles the most cited authors were then researched to create a database in excess of 2,000* relevant peer reviewed journal papers which were reviewed for relevance.

3.3 Research background

Published works prior to the Mid 80s refers more to strategy and management decision making than working with others and sees management working alone to reach organisational goals. The literature published in the mid 80s to mid 90s discusses more about the profit and gains from alliances and refers to them as joint ventures which suggests more a meeting of business structures than people collaborating for mutual benefit. During the latter part of the 20th century we see a shift and more terminology such as strategic alliances and the understanding that by exploiting core capabilities and pooling resources cooperating firms can achieve common goals. This may be in response to the need for business structures to change as the environment and technology demands Mandal et al (2003) this is corroborated in the study by Sarkis et al (2007) as they develop a model that allows for virtual partner selection.

We continue to see a shift in the literature as it relates to collaboration and trust Adobor (2006) where uncertainty can be a determinant and also limit the amount of trust placed on a partner, it is indicated that strategic management of the alliance can also reduce distrust. This in turn generates literature that focuses on alliance objectives and models of collaboration including theory of cooperation Teng and Das (2008); Todeva and Knoke (2005) i.e. long term goals rather than turn around profit, acknowledging management experience Teng and Das (2008)

The latter part of the decade has focused on the dynamics and evolution of these relationships and the reasons why partners are chosen, this is done by learning about the "actual decision making processes" Pidduck (2009 pp 262). Further understanding of the key factors in partner selection is building on earlier works around classifications of business alliances strategies (Jarratt, 1999). It is also at this time that researchers acknowledge that the customer and supplier have resources and capabilities that can be utilised by cooperation (Soosay et al, 2008).

At the same time theory building and research turns to innovation and how applying it to R&D in a virtual environment serves as a strategic business tool (Holtzman, 2008; Sarkis et al, 2007).

Despite this chronological categorising of research into the book topic areas it is acknowledged that during each period researchers have seen ahead and discussed or highlighted the need for research into other fields while in some cases researchers have been the pioneer in certain research areas identifying the need for interdisciplinary research and corroboration and collaboration. Deeds et al (1999); Jarratt (1998); Pidduck (2006); Mandal et al (2003)

It can be argued that the aim of strategic alliance research is to create knowledge about the perceptions, motivations and drivers for SAs and the outcomes and this knowledge can be classified as either having a practical outcome or making a methodological contribution to knowledge.

Practical contributions to knowledge documents historical and contemporary research and their results in particular those having practical importance, value, or effect on alliance formulation.

Methodological contributions to knowledge are those which indicate areas of future research needs and also discusses tools and methods used to arrive at the current knowledge, often discussing at length the success or failure of certain models Todeva & Knoke (2005).

It is acknowledged that research carried out by various authors that they have promoted successful cases and models whereas they do not discuss those that fail especially in terms of increasing knowledge for producing prescriptive solutions for the future. This may be an attempt to protect their interests and current or future research projects. Synthesis this research will assist in developing a model that is more prescriptive for the future in partner selection and the resultant growth of the firm and as a consequence the industry sector.

The literature review offers a critical review of prior research relevant to Strategic Alliance formation and collaboration in SMEs and more specifically those in high tech or high growth industries who may form alliances related to Research and Development.

Research has tended to cover one industry sector which may have excluded possible successful ventures or created in bias in the research, at the same time there may need to be a paradigm shift or classification of what construes a high tech or high growth firm.

3.4 Background to high tech SMEs

High tech industries are considered those that produce sophisticated products but not always of a technological nature, although there is a significant emphasis on research and development which can require the use of technology or technological components for example telecommunications. Within academic research the terms such as high tech, high growth etc often are used interchangeably and industry classifications will be dealt with elsewhere. High tech firms are invariably found on science or technology parks often with association to an academic institute or private funding to create a supportive business environment. Gower and Harris (1996) assert that occupancy levels have remained steady. The number of parks that are members of United Kingdom Science Park Association (UKSPA) have grown from 40 in the early 1990s to over 164 in 2008.

An aim of this literature review is to gain an understanding of terminology used within and between SMEs in the high tech industries located in technology and science parks and the application of strategic management frameworks in the formation of their alliances. The review examines contemporary and historical literature around alliances, networking and collaborative technologies and organizational learning. Strategic alliance terminology is not easily defined in the literature as authors often assume prior knowledge by the reader, therefore this literature review will also contribute to chapter two where clarification of topics and subject areas are given.

3.5 Key themes

The key themes to this research are dealt with one by one to try and hypothesise the literature to give a clear background to the research. To enable this the review is split into the various research areas which are related to this book. The review will firstly look at strategy development in organisations which is the research area that this book relates to as is strategic alliance formation and management. Review will take place of the motivations and drivers for forming strategic alliances over other types of partnering.

Secondly the review will look at the empirical work on Strategic Alliances, collaborations and inter-firm cooperation to better understand the way academics and practitioners approach the use and theory of strategic alliances.

The third section of the literature review will explore the models and conceptual frameworks developed by researchers into the study of the high tech high growth firms and industries to assist in understanding what has already been presented and also as stated elsewhere this book is not intended to reinvent the wheel but to build on the excellent models already available.

The fourth section looks at organisational structure and strategic alliance development in particular management characteristics, including age, work experience, educational attainment and prior partnering experiences which influence the decisions they make about working with others.

Finally bringing the reviewed areas together will highlight the gap in literature and based on this analysis the development of a research methodology and conceptual framework or model to answer the research question.

3.6 Strategic management, alliance development and management

3.6.1 Strategic management

Strategic management as an academic field is relatively young compared to some disciplines Stonehouse and Pemberton (2002) despite this observation strategic management in industrial SMEs was in evidence (Berg, 1985, Chapple, 1999; More, 2000) and is now widely researched a tribute to its importance for business growth and the need for business to plan strategically all aspects of the business including choosing to collaborate with competitors (Singh et al, 2008).

"Strategy is the direction and scope of an organization over the long term which achieves advantage in a changing environment through its configuration of resources and competences with the aim of fulfilling stakeholder expectations"(Johnson et al 2008 p3) "the means by which the enterprise achieves its objectives" Morden (2007;ch11 p184) Therefore those firms who seek alliances are making best use of the resources and competences of its partners firms in which it lacks. Arguably a strategic alliance may describe how a number of partners are going to work together when in reality what they actually do is something different i.e. developing trust where it is only the perception of trust to enable gain.

Strategic alliances in particular help organisations to compete during environmental changes and turbulence by giving them access to resources that will help them extend their business

74

through such developments as creating new opportunities and also enhancing business capabilities while utilising those of their suppliers, customers and even competitors through alliances (Soosay et al, 2008; Calof and Wright, 2008).

Strategic alliance as an academic field has been widely researched however the reasons for specific alliances and the resultant success of these alliances is less researched despite significant increases in the volume of literature produced during the last decade Hoffman et al (1996). Historically Hoffman et al (1996) argued that despite an impressive SME literature it does not "provide robust, conclusive answers" within the field of high tech high growth industry and they draw attention to some areas of neglect and it is seen from researchers such as (Hagedoorn, 2002; Aggarwal and Hsu; 2009) who claim that there is a need to corroborate literature to explain the phenomenon and acknowledge it is more widely researched a tribute to its importance for business growth as newer firms seek alliances to enable integration with downstream activities, Contemporary literature has begun to question who alliances benefit as more established firms seek cooperation between numerous partners.

3.6.2 Defining strategic alliances

A vast historical selection of literature on business strategy and alliances focuses on larger organizations and it is difficult to use these as benchmarks for SMEs, (Thakkar et al, 2008; Byars; 1987) Vyas et al, (1995 p47) argues that the option to remain independent for SMEs is no longer viable and strategic alliances previously the domain of "corporate giants" strategic alliances are seen as an essential part of strategic management and strategy formulation for sustainability and growth.

75

Literature that analyses SMEs and strategy tends to be directed at manufacturing organizations for example see (Barnes, 2001; Garengo et al, 2005; Garengo and Bititci, 2007; Karami, 2007; O'Regan et al, 2008) and those researchers that aim at the high tech high growth sector have focused on the scope of R&D alliances (Oxley and Sampson, 2004). Knowledge Access and Transfer (Petruzzelli et al, 2007; Marshall, 2008). Factors influencing partner selection (Shah and Swaminathan, 2008; Rothaermel and Boeker, 2008) management capabilities (Deeds et al, 1999; Schreiner et al, 2008; Lin et al, 2009; Arikan and MCGahan, 2010) and as a tribute to the need to understand organisational culture and its impact on alliances and changes that occur internally as a result (Leisen et al, 2002; Pansiri 2005) further corroborated by Ghosh (2004) who asserts that organisational learning is not the sum of each of its members individual learning. This links the literature about organisational learning with that of understanding the dynamic capabilities of a firm and how this differs from a resource based view of a firm.

The view that strategic alliance and small business growth literature is lacking in conformity possibly stems from the perspective of the researchers and the research questions they are answering. Other authors focus on the mode of collaboration and the drivers for this for example Aggarwal and Hsu (2009).

The growing importance of understanding the motives of SMEs to form alliances and its importance in the economy that has spurred theory and research to adopt multiple measures of research. It is also reported by some that despite a growth in inter firm cooperation or alliances there is still a high rate of failures (Gulati et al, 2008)

There are many definitions of strategic alliances however they usually relate to two or more partner firms (Todeva and Knoke, 2005) or can consist of multiple partners with complex agreements (Niren et al, 1995). While working with each other in some markets they may be competing in others this paradox of competition and co-operation known as co-option is widely researched (Clarke-Hill et al, 2003).

Definitions have remained fairly consistent over the decades with a general consensus that strategic alliances are formed to assist with improving time to market and reducing costs. Within this consistency are complex differentiators and allowances made for industrial segments, environmental turmoil and customer needs not to mention competition from emerging economies and the ability to mass produce and market of large MNEs whose ability to forward and backward integrate reduces costs, increases core competencies.

According to Hagedoorn (1993 Ch6 pp 116)

"strategic technology alliances are to be understood as those inter-firm cooperative agreements aimed at improving the long-term perspective of the product market combination of at least one of the companies involved".

Niren et al (1995 p47)

"any relationship between companies involving a sharing of common destinies" "A strategic alliance is an agreement between two or more partners to share knowledge or resources which could be beneficial to all parties involved

From these early dates view points have changed and fifteen years on according to Johnson et al (2008 Ch 10 pp 360) Who speaks more generally

" a strategic alliance is where two or more organisations share resources and activities to pursue a strategy"

Todeva and Knoke (2005) make the following points

- Remain legally independent after the alliance is formed
- Share benefits and managerial control over the performance of assigned tasks and
- Make continuing contributions in one or more strategic areas, such as technology or products and can relate to many different aspects of a firm e.g human resources often considered the most important resource Johnson et al (2008)

Jarratt (1998;pp39) give the following definition

"pooling of specific resources and skills by the cooperating organisations in order to achieve common goals as well as goals specific to the individual partners"

The chronology of these works indicates that the increase in the number of high tech high growth SMEs and their role in the economy has generated an interest in them as a separate species having a set of particular needs, goals, and aims and objectives which differ from non high tech firms and service sector firms. The means by which they achieve their goals may not be the same strategy frameworks employed by larger firms within the same industries nor those of non high tech SMEs.

Despite the increasing number of studies and research on strategic alliances of SMEs and their partners there is not enough robust information on which to conclude that businesses who form strategic alliances and interfirm cooperation choose partners wisely and are successful and grow. The literature review has bought three main focuses of academics when talking about high tech SMEs; cooperation, strategy and growth and my research will reflect these.

3.6.3 Alliance as a relationship

The use of terms such as relationship or alliances between firms has not been well defined and while in Marketing terms building relationships is well researched it is less covered in a strategic sense and research has tried to link the two Jarratt (1998).

Most firms have a large number of relationships which rely on unequal contributions e.g. banks, suppliers, governmental departments unlike an alliance where the contribution and outcome should be equal and in particular in relation to this book where the research will concentrate on the formation of strategic alliances including technology cooperation as defined by Hagerdoon (1993) where an exchange of technology is paramount to the phenomenon. The review briefly mentions but will not dwell on inter-firm cooperation that relates to only marketing or financial cooperation. Despite this assertion it is understood by the researcher that to collaborate successfully other aspects of inter-firm cooperation may be needed (Calof and Wright, 2008).

Researchers have been interested in the motivations and drivers for strategic alliances and have a diverse catalogue of reasons however one of the key factors in strategic alliances is the development of new products and the ability to get them to market and is viewed as a key determinant of success (Deeds et al, 1999). Not all firms have the capabilities or resources to be all things for example an innovative company lacks the ability to market its products or even meet demand due to limited production facilities.

Literature deals with a number of issues regarding strategic alliance formation. On the one hand there is networking either formally encouraged by incubator management or less formally organised by firms with similar specialisations or characteristics. In these two instances no exchange of services or products take place on the other hand there are formal inter firm exchanges often consisting of intricate legal dialogues to protect both (or multiple) firms. Despite this legal protection it will be seen later that one firm can gain less than the other when one actively seeks to gain a competitive advantage through its ability to exploit a newer less experienced firm or those who have not yet learnt to protect their core competences (Gulati et al, 2009).

3.6.4 Motivations for seeking alliances

Literature offers a number of perspectives on how and why companies seek alliances, and within these theories there are two clear views one is that companies adopt an organisational view or a resource based view, and the requirements or opportunities within a firm may dictate which approach they take.

Alliances can be sought for the mutual benefit of firms and can assist new firms in obtaining stability and reputation while an established firm may obtain innovative ideas and approaches.

It is asserted that that the rapid development of new products is seen as a key feature of success Deeds et al (1999) however less research focuses on how firms are to achieve this when they lack a combination of economic resources, hold little or no competitive advantages and due often to lack of age and experience have little organisational learning with which to exploit any advantages they have in innovative practices. It can be seen therefore that motivations for forming strategic alliances and more explicitly the need for strategic management in formulation surround gaining access to complementary assets for example knowledge, increasing the activities that the firm is engaged in and by sharing risk and cost can increase speed of productivity and distribution. It is important however to know when to use these alliances as a competitive weapon (Drago, 1997).

3.6.5 Policy making and alliances

Through literature review it can be seen that SMEs are increasingly seen as an important catalyst for economic growth. Policy makers are becoming more interested in the operations and processes of SMEs however the amount of support and knowledge sharing can vary from region to region.

It is asserted that firms form alliances and have strategies in place to support them however through the literature it is not clear how the promotion and facilitation of these alliances is carried out and what policies exist to assist them.

3.6.6 Factors in success or failure of strategic alliances

The number of alliances that are cemented is not clear as often informal agreements are made neither is it clear why some firms seek alliances rather than look inward for resources while even more give more to the alliance than they receive, whether there is mutual or equal benefit to both parties in the alliance. If one firm has a stronger position than the other that firm then becomes open to abuse of the trust it places in its partner firms or it may not be possible to measure the long term benefits (Teece 1986; Tyler, 2001; Lunnan and Haugland, 2008) nor to determine whether termination of an alliance is due to failure or success.

Furthermore it can be argued that repeatedly forming alliances with the same partners could result in them obtaining a proprietary interest in the firm and as a result the information they access is greater than that which they give. According to Gulati et al (2009) this increases the risk of opportunistic behaviour.

It is understood that prior partnering experiences can have an affect on future alliances and may influence or contribute to value creation. It is important to note that repeated re partnering suggests a more stable alliance and according to Gulati (2009 pp1214) "provides greater benefits than general partnering experience". Meanwhile Greiner (1972) asserts that a companies prior experiences are critical to their future success, there are nearly 30 years between these two writings however they both assert that experience is key to future decision making.

3.6.7 Core competencies and competitive advantage

As firms face more challenges in todays' economic turbulence they find it difficult to achieve and maintain competitive advantage. Literature presents models that prescribe how firms can by using their technological innovation and the ability to develop trusting relationships based on prior experiences to achieve competitive advantage which can not be replicated nor can be achieved by competitors for their own gain (Tyler 2001; Mandal et al, 2003).

The internal capabilities may affect how a business is willing to build its relationship when it outsources, outsourcing according to Espino-Rodriguez and Rodriguez-Diaz (2008) is becoming an important phenomena which contributes to competitive advantage. They further propose that outsourcing is "a particular form of strategic alliance" corroborated by Zinelding and Bredenlow (2003) who examine the particular difficulties faced with organisations when outsourcing due to the fact that often it is seen as only the acquisition of products and services outside the business.

To exploit its core capabilities a firm should invest in activities where it is competent and outsource the rest this differs from the view of strategic alliances where both firms exchange their capabilities for mutual benefit.

Seminal literature has been on the increase of service industries and it would appear that there has been a servicing growth within high tech industries. McIvor (2000) asserts that organisations are moving away from what were previously concerned with outsourcing such as cleaning or security to outsourcing of key elements for example component manufacturing, logistics, design and R&D including the complete production and assembly of goods by third parties resulting in some firms becoming specialist in coordinating rather than production corroboration comes from Busi and McIvor (2008). Outsourcing decision making can be seen as strategic however research has not illustrated the dangers of over reliance on outsourcing as opposed to strategic alliance where it is generally anticipated that trust and mutual gain are instrumental.

Capabilities come with time and experience therefore an exploration of how firms develop capabilities is required, while they may form strategic alliances to improve their competencies what do they have to offer a partner?

3.6.8 Applying strategy to alliance development

Applying strategy in partner selection (Mellet-Parast and Digman, 2007; Dealtry, 2008; Chen et al; 2008; Lin and Lin, 2010; Jones et al, 2003). Perhaps the chronology of these suggests that academics and practitioners both realise the importance of strategically planning and manageing alliances for competitive advantage, growth rather than relying on old partnerships which may have outlived their usefulness, no longer be acceptable to the consumer and in the particular area of Corporate Social Responsibility (CSR) consumers are more worried about where their goods and services have come from than the cost.

Teng and Das (2008 pp725) propose that the choices on the structure of the alliances may be shaped by factors such as "joint R&D and joint marketing objectives, alliance management experience, and international partners" this suggests an alliance based on similar needs rather than seeking out partners whose weaknesses are your areas of strength Tyler (2001). It may further explain the decision to undertake joint ventures rather than a contractual alliance.

3.7 Explore the models and conceptual frameworks

While alliances have to be contemporary and flexible historical models and concepts are important in creating a framework for modern thinking and for the purpose of this study have been fundamental in creating this literature review strategy.

According to Leshem and Trafford (2007) it is not often clear what relevance a conceptual framework has to other research, and also what is required in one. They argue that it is possible that the framework evolves as research continues. It is also proposed that as concepts are not tangible where as a framework is solid and things can be presented within its boundaries then a conceptual framework is a contradiction. The development of my model will be based on the frameworks, concepts and paradigms of others and the concept or idea will be developed to produce a framework.

The models reviewed in the early stages of the literature review are diverse but are not examined in light of their reliability etc but on the diverse nature they are focused. The purpose of modelling is discussed together with some of the problems with justifying findings. The intended model in this book does not resemble other popular business models for measuring performance or effectiveness such as the balance scorecard. Through the literature it is seen that many of the models proposed are limited as they are unable to measure anything other than financial aspects of organisational performance.

3.7.1 Using models to explain phenomena

Following in the trend of the literature the frameworks and models are focused on; understanding the outsourcing process for the management of services for example see (McIvor, 2000; Hassanain and Al-Saadi, 2005).

Creating models for technology alliance explaining how organisational learning enables competitive advantage through alliances (Ju et al, 2005) meanwhile Dealtry (2008 p 443) explores further the business factors that shape best practices in the management of strategic alliances. He asserts that there is a naivety in the assumption that relationships work well for both parties and says "models for success are readily available".

Research and Development collaboration according to Philbin (2008) is important to enable understanding of this phenomena and it is also important that research is focused on operational and decision making using other quality measurement models (Leonard and McAdam, 2002), this enables SME managers to produce a strategy and build relationships which work for them. And finally a new focus in management and studies and for business understanding a need to evaluate partner selection in reverse logistics which also impacts on the amount of materials used in the forward system (Meade and Sarkis, 2002), this helps reduce costs and enables relationship building at any stage of the process.

In relation to management perceptions and organisational learning the objective of this section of the review is to ascertain the extent that management perceptions, organisational structures and learning affect successful alliances formulation for example see (Leisen et al, 2002; Pansiri, 2005).

Organisational development impacts on alliance formation when each one have their own individual problems, competition and restrictions due to political climates and research has been diverse on these topics trying to provide synergy to enable best practice for SMEs for example see (French 2004b; Glaister et al 2008; Dobbs & Hamilton 2007; Moriarty and Jones 2008; Kraus et al 2006; Meeham & Lindsey 2008; Johnston et al 2008; O'Regan et al 2008; Pasanen & Laukkanen 2006; Singh et al 2008). According to Pillania (2009) strategy is still a concept that is subject to interpretation and he points out that the use formulation and implementation is down to individual managers. It is also implied in the literature that when a company maintains it has a strategy expectations are held that there is a plan available which is infallible and if followed success is assured and this assumption will be followed when creating the model.

Human resource is considered a most important resource Johnson et al (2008) and in particular the role of strategic managers and their ability to deploy resources and build relationships, furthermore they discuss relationships outside the firm such as outsourcing and strategic alliances, any type of relationship building should be done in the understanding of how quickly change takes place, knowledge sharing and increased internationalisation.

3.7.2 Motivations for seeking an alliance

The reputation and legitimacy of an organisation can be considered an asset of a firm and in doing so it must be considered that the two are inseperable and are of equal importance when forming alliances therefore legitimacy as an asset can be seen to make the company more competitive if others are not seen to have the same asset, It is argued that by association a firm can obtain resources of an intangible nature such as reputation. It is argued that by pooling complementary skills i.e. young firms with new innovative ideas and established firms with management and developmental know how can bring products to market quicker and cheaper than either company can do so alone.

Motivation for seeking strategic alliances will differ for each firm however as identified by Johnson et al there are infrastructure alliances that involve the shaping of resources and do not give any firm opportunity to gain competitive advantage on the other hand more and more strategic alliances consist of each firm seeking to gain such an advantage motivations for this type of alliance are;-

The need for critical mass achieved by creating partnerships which lead to cost reductions through the provision of complementary services or products. According to Gulati et al (2009) costs can be reduced when alliances are created with known partners. Working with known partners can also reduce the possibility of conflict and reduces uncertainty. This is not to say that all recurring partnerships will work (Park and Kim (1997).

Each firm has an activity or core competence the other firm does not have i.e. R&D facilities, local knowledge. Use of other firms in their forward or backward integration processes commonly known as co-specialisation when one firms abilities complements anothers.

- For learning – Firms who cooperate develop competencies that they can take into other partnerships or alliances

- According to Todeva and Knoke (2005) who expand on the work of Agarwal "The strategic motives for organisations to engage in alliance formation vary according to firm specific characteristics and the multiple environmental factors." The diverse range of reasons for seeking alliance includes;

- Distribution channels, Economies of scale, Overcoming legal/regulatory barriers, Sharing of resources to reduce costs

Deciding to form an alliance or cooperate with another firm is not the result of action taken to be reactive but is more likely to be a strategic decision to improve the long term efficiencies and standing of the firm. According to Todeva and Knoke (2005) there are four levels at which the motivations and drivers for strategic alliances are enacted;

- Organisational
- economic,
- strategic,
- political

Wanting to carry out a R&D project for which it is resource and knowledge under subscribed then a firm may consider forming an alliance, Oxley & Sampson (2004) this is an attractive solution however deciding who to form an alliance with may pose many difficulties for the manager. Deciding which firms to create an alliance with may only be the beginning of the dilemma as the manager also has to consider who will undertake which tasks and which parts of the business should be subjected to the alliance. They may want to be open and honest and create a trusting environment however they will also want to protect their knowledge from excessive leakage. Firms have to decide at which stage of their operation they wish to undertake their alliance.

3.7.3 Frequency and quality of alliances

Since 1993 the number of strategic alliances have more than doubled (Zineldin and Bredenlow, 2003) however the number that actually survive can be as low as 30% and this is cited as stemming from implementation problems or simply from poor relationship and Zineldin and Bredenlow (2003) suggest that there is a basic criteria which is needed to be successful and they cite that it is equally important to develop trust and communication as well as displaying strategic management (Drago, 1997).

The above citations suggest that further analysis of the reasons for failure need to be done as while drawbacks of alliances resulting in failure is hypothesised as being a lack of trust, lack of common goals (Drago, 1997) then there is a need for more prescriptive measures in selecting partners i.e. those partners who have similar goals, ethics etc..

3.7.4 The paradox of competitor and collaborator

Literature does not expand on the competitive effects of alliances, it is suggested that if companies are competitive at market level then they may not share wholly, taking knowledge without sharing their own, (Oxley and Sampson, 2004) this does not mean that successful R&D ventures do not happen but it is suggested by Khanna et al (1998) that each firm will participate in cooperative behaviour and competitive behaviour. However for many there are issues of trust when competitors begin to collaborate for further examples of the paradox of competition and cooperation (Bogers, 2011).

3.7.5 Firms evolutionary and revolutionary processes

As organisations grow their need and or reliance on partnering will differ according to Greiner (1972) organisations go through five stages of development while others have looked at the stages of growth. As discussed by authors if small companies choose an inappropriate structure they will be acquired by a bigger firm when they fail, in a similar way if a firm chooses an inappropriate partner for an alliance they are likely to be open to sabotage, theft of its designs and poor productivity.

The range of empirical work relating to the models for strategic alliances has been reviewed together with research to investigating the use of these models and the resultant successes. Two types of empirical research have been identified in current literature those that carry out new field work and that which used existing government sourced data and analysed it using controlling factors. The work of Hagardoon had been particularly influential in the area of modes of cooperation in high tech industries. Hagardoon by concentrating on technology cooperation has been able to highlight the difficulties in defining strategic alliances especially in terms of organisational behaviour.

There appears to be little empirical research into the impact of state intervention on alliance formation (Todeva and Knoke, 2005) however when it is seen the extent to which they intervene in incubation sites this suggests that they are instrumental in the early success or failure of high tech firms, university or corporate spinoffs fair differently when seeking alliances because of their inherent culture and their experiences as start ups (Kumararamangalam, 2005).

3.8 Managers perceptions and strategic alliance formulation

In reviewing strategic alliances it is important to understand the role of leadership or managers in the formulation of alliances as according to Porter (1996) "....a clear strategy is often primarily an organisational one and depends on leadership." It is primarily understood that the prior experiences and expectations of managers will influence their behaviour in the future

The review takes an objective but critical look at the more recent literature and its importance for successful alliance management. It will investigate the proposition that success is not only measured in terms of financial gain but also the strength of the alliance and the trust and long term relationship that is formed. These relationships are shaped by prior experiences and this knowledge is not something that is easily gained and means that knowledge in an organisation is a competitive advantage. Lasch et al (2007) hypothesise that growth is positively related to the working experience of the entrepreneur however was not able to prove this and explained that other firm specificities may have been excluded.

3.9 Controlling the alliances

According to Hoffman et al (1996) "recent policymaking has been directed" at innovation in SMES and infrastructures have developed with EU expansion to assist this. These industries continue to evolve impacted on by environmental and technology as well as facing challenges created by policy makers, economic problems. For many of these firms fast technological advances have bought benefits in terms of faster production, marketing etc there will have been downsides for example the cost of new technology, training etc which may be prohibitive to some small SMEs also competitors will also experience the same benefits one way of overcoming these problems is to seek alliances (Lin and Darling, 1999)

3.9.1 The process and value of undertaking strategic alliances

Byars (1987) suggests there are two stages to SM decision making and implementation while Jauch (1988) suggests that it is usually carried out as three separate functions; choice, implementation, and evaluation. Research shows that there is evidence in the records of strategic planning businesses that they expand more often than those who use strategic or financial control (Goold and Cambell, 1987). This is corroborated by Porter (1996). Strategic Alliance is no different it is necessary to identify a need for the alliance to choose a partner, implement the alliance and then to evaluate it

A problem with creating an alliance is that following the time of agreement things do not remain static and there is a risk that before the strategy has been fully implemented problems may occur. Mintzberg (1987b) proposes that it is difficult to decide a long term plan and that strategies which emerge over time is the best way for modern companies, this suggests that less formal and maybe informal networking would be a better process. As discussed elsewhere this may be down to the characteristics and preferences of individual mangers Mullins (2005).

3.10 Chapter summary

The main objective of this literature review was to identify key research issues around high tech industries however defined. Not all the studies discussed in this literature review are relevant to this study however there are some emerging themes which enables the researcher to identify areas that are primed for research.

Despite the increasing number of studies and research on all the research topic areas there was not enough robust information on which to conclude that partnering criteria is prescriptive and understood by practitioners. It was therefore deemed important to undertake research into manager's motivation and perception of strategic alliance.

Evaluation of existing frameworks have highlighted some of minor relevant relevance to entrepreneurial businesses today. However it is also deemed necessary to find or create new models to suit the entrepreneurial spirit of these organic businesses as alluded to by French (2004).

The literature has not presented any agreements about what are key factors in either the success or failure of high tech industry firms. As strategic alliance is put forward as a strategy that enables firms to be innovative, carry out R&D and as a result grow the lack of empirical research on how these alliances have failed has promoted the need to create models that can predict success through correct partnering selection.

Prior research into success and failure of alliance have not conformed to a criteria therefore method and results have been different and can not be compared for a consensus, it is seen however that there is a propensity for high failure rates as recorded by some studies in these industries despite the increasing number of start ups.

Frequently the research and consequently the focus of the literature is on one industry sector or explores the process of the alliance for example ICT Lasch et al (2007) biotechnology sector Kumaramangalam (2006). Of those that have measured strategic alliance all the researchers have indicated that there are a number of variables that influence the success or failure of a strategic alliance and these include manager's experiences, criteria for partner selection and critical success factors for the alliance Chen and Karami (2010).

The literature review highlights that alliance formulation decision is an important aspect of alliance management and needs to balance how the alliance is structured to ensure the protection of a firms' knowledge and assets. The majority of the research has been carried out in emerging countries where high exportation of technology is experienced, the experiences of companies in the UK are different and are less researched, although more companies start life in incubator or technology parks and rely more on inter-firm cooperation when they face the business world alone. Research is limited to established firms while organic start-ups and incubator projects are less explored. Writers during the past three decades have emphasised the increase in inter-firm technology during consecutive decades (Hagerdoorn, 1993; Gulati et al, 2009) therefore it is not time to look at the motivation for these partnerships.

Chapter Four: Synthesis of Literature and Development of Conceptual Framework

4.1 Introduction

This chapter presents the conceptual framework to further investigate the research objectives and research propositions in synthesis with the literature review detailed in chapter three. This will enable chapter five to develop a suitable methodology for the research.

4.2 Conceptual framework

The conceptual framework introduces the dependant and independent variables, the hypothesis and the relationship between them. It constructs the structures which classify subjects and enable the researcher to organise thinking and create a plan of action Rowley and Slack (2004). Authors have used the terms conceptual framework and theoretical framework to represent the same thing and at times the literature review is used to present the agenda for study Merriam and Simpson (2000, pp. 10) suggest that the literature review is "to develop a conceptual framework or to explore a topical area of study". On the other hand Leshem and Trafford (2007, p 97)

> "present a case for the conceptual framework to fulfil two roles: firstly, providing a theoretical clarification of what researchers intend to investigate, and, secondly, enabling readers to be clear what the research seeks to achieve, and how that will be achieved".

It could be argued however that the literature review covers both theory and methods used by previous researchers and that they while being similar are different steps in creating the book.

According to Rocco and Plakhotnik (2009) there are five steps that the literature review and conceptual and theoretical frameworks cover and suggest that whether a literature review or framework where used then the results would be the same.

- To lay the foundations of the book, by using previous work to illustrate trends in research and findings and provide an overview of previous concepts.
- Indicates the contribution to knowledge by highlighting the gaps in existing studies and generating and clarifying possible research questions
- Conceptualise own ideas by looking at theoretical frameworks
- Create research and design frame work
- Provide references to enable discussion and analysis of findings.

4.2.1 Components of conceptual framework

Prior to developing the conceptual framework it is important to analyse the key themes discussed in chapters two and three in light of the research objectives and prior research to identify potential key variables.

The importance of SMEs to the economy are well documented and the importance of planning and strategic management are well researched for larger firms the SMEs have been neglected. There are arguments regarding the benefit of planning to SMEs and at best they are seen as informal planners. Furthermore literature in the arena of high tech industries and particularly alliances is equally scarce and while management role is

100

critical in SMEs there role is still not widely researched in developing and employing strategies. Therefore recognising the gaps in literature this study has raised some questions to address these shortfalls.

4.3 Defining the manager

All areas of SMEs are usually controlled by the manager who is responsible for making all the operational decisions. These terms manager owner and entrepreneur are used interchangeably in literature with some authors clearly dividing the two. Schumpeter (1934) thought that being innovative was what set the entrepreneur apart from an SME owner further authors have argued that it is the exploitation of ideas that sets an entrepreneur apart. Sole trader, sole worker, self employed are all terms associated with new start up but entrepreneurial activity are put forward by Schumpeter (1934) as being characterised by:

- Introduction of new goods
- Introduction of new methods of production
- Opening of new markets
- Opening of new sources of supply
- Industrial reorganisation

4.3.1 Management strategies

Businesses whose objectives include survival and growth usually form a plan this can either be formal or informal. For SMEs in the high tech industry how they should plan is not clear as their priorities may change from product driven to market driven over a period of time. Historical literature has failed to address the needs of the SME however they all concede that the role of the manager (entrepreneur) is important in achieving organisational goals. In literature there is a suggestion that the types of strategy undertaken is down to the entrepreneur's or owner's personality, however Schumpeter asserts that once an entrepreneur works on the business then he is then a manager there is collaboration for this from Thompson (1999).

Through a review of historical and contemporary literature I propose another definition of entrepreneur which could also refer to a manager of an organic business.

> "an entrepreneur is any one willing to take a risk of starting an organic business in these economic times, whether they remain a sole trader, take on employees or replicate existing businesses."

4.3.2 Management variables

Hair et al (2007 p144) defines variables as:

> "An independent variable is a measureable characteristic that influenced or explains the dependent variable.
> A dependent variable is ... the variable you are trying to understand, explain or predict".

4.3.3 Management behaviour

As discussed firms do not exist in isolation they are run by managers who bring with them characteristics which will impact on their decision making abilities and preferences. For this reason a managers perception of his environment influences his decision making, management demographics and prior experience are therefore important independent variables.

4.3.4 Defining management variables

SME managers have to perform in similar ways to conduct their business, however their individual demographics and background characteristics i.e. gender, age, education, managerial experience have been chosen as the independent variables for analysis of the data collected during the empirical research. Analysing these variables will enable profiling of managers and testing the hypothesis. These variables have been chosen by prior researchers as important when studying SMEs for example see (Cui and Mak, 2002; Carmen et al, 2006). Similarly, identifying the characteristics of the firms is important as the size, age and industry will impact on the firm performance. Prior alliance has focused on the type of strategy undertaken and reasons for failure and for some the factors that are critical to the success which includes motivation for the alliance (Chen and Karami, 2010), these are the variables considered for this study.

To answer the research question and address research objective one questions related to management demographics formed section one of the questionnaire.

Hypothesis one is associated with finding correlation between managers demographic and strategic alliance success. Information about age, gender, education, length of tenure. Age is expected to be correlated with taking risks and younger managers may be more of a risk taker however older managers may be more experienced and avoid alliances due to prior experience. Education is considered an indication of overall ability and capability however it also has to be acknowledged that older managers may have tacit knowledge developed over time.

Empirical research using demographic variables have been found to be reliable sources of information about managers and their behaviour.

According to Goll et al (2008 pp 206)

"While not perfect substitutes for the underlying constructs, demographic variables offer the advantage of being objective testable and Comprehensive". They find support that links demographic variables to strategy and performance".

Figure 4.1 presents an example where strategic alliance success is a dependant variable affected by the independent variable of managerial demographics. These variables are used to test hypothesis one. These view the effect that managerial demographics i.e. gender, age, education and managerial experience have on alliance success. These variables have been used successfully by prior researchers as it is supported that these characteristics heavily influence the firms performance for example see (Weinshall and Vickery, 1987: Catley and Hamilton, 1998: Kathuria and Porth, 2003: Wu and Callahan, 2005: Carmen et al, 2006: Karami et al, 2006: Granrose, 2007: Massey and Dawes, 2007: Ndemo and Maina, 2007: Goll et al, 2008: Cohoon et al, 2010: Yordanova and Alexandrova-Boshnakova, 2011: Zhang and Bruning, 2011).

Figure 4.1 Independent and dependant variables used to test hypothesis one

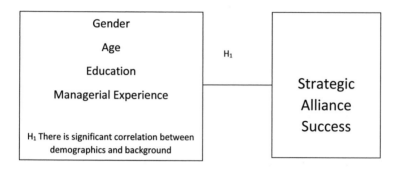

Gender		
Age	H_1	
Education		Strategic
Managerial Experience		Alliance
		Success
H_1 There is significant correlation between demographics and background		

Independent Variable

Independent variables   Dependant Variable

According to Easterby smith et al (2008) when there is an association between two variables knowing how someone scores on one variable can help predict how they might respond on another.

As can be seen management and firm demographics may impact on all other aspects of the firm. There is a strong link in literature between management demographics, strategic management or decision making and firm performance (Goll et al, 2008). There is little evidence to date that firms and managerial demographics impact on strategic alliances and these are more likely to be caused by other drivers. The conceptual model presented in this research builds on that of Goll et al (2008 pp 206) who propose that "the environment moderates the relationship between top management characteristics and strategy as well as the relationship between strategy and performance. Their study revolved around the airline industry and focused on the combined characteristics of top management teams however it supports and is supported by other literature and based on this I propose

"that managerial and firm demographics have a positive effect

on decision making and the employment of strategic management tools

which in turn impacts on strategic alliance formation and success".

The philosophy behind this assumption is that an alliance is born from management planning, based on the analysis that is carried out by the manager. A managers' propensity to strategically manage the firm comes from their demographics. They do not happen as a result of crisis but are born from sound strategy, the high failure rate is explained by lack of understanding of the partnering firms' motivations and the inability to monitor and evaluate the alliance.

4.4 Defining SMEs

Small to medium sized businesses a topic of high interest by academics for decades. These firms are said to be accountable for significant job creation in the UK. There is no one defining reason for this however it is widely debated in literature see for example (Jones-Evans and Westhead 1996:) Industrial and sector figures vary and it is difficult to find data sets of high tech SMEs currently operating in the UK. This appears to be for a number of reasons:

- Figures are collated from different sources and there is conflict between those cited by OECD, eurostat and ONS, this is partly due to the measurements used and partly due to groupings of industrial areas and country activity. More recently the government has been focusing on activity in the M4 corridor while universities collaborate and research with science or other parks in their area. When university's research focus on the firms in their location and with whom they collaborate, non collaborating firms etc are excluded.

- The OECD publishes figures however these are based on GDPs and do not indicate the number of businesses operating. Furthermore SMEs are not required to be registered for VAT and PAYE under certain thresholds and those who register with companies' house do so to reduce risk to the owner and not for the purpose of supplying data although there is some requirement for returns to be submitted.

- Researchers have stated "data on the absolute number of high technology firm births and deaths cannot be presented because it is not currently published" Jones-Evans and Kirby (1993). In 2008 The Department for Business Enterprise and Regulatory Reform (BERR) published a paper which only focused on the high growth firms many of which are found in the high tech sector. "High growth firms are found to contribute a disproportionate amount to employment growth. High growth firms also display higher levels of productivity than average. This combination of high productivity and employment growth implies that high growth firms are responsible for a substantial proportion of economic growth." While these share some characteristics with high tech firms they are not necessarily one and the same.

The research into high tech firms and the number of incidences of these firms has been concentrated in the 1990s (Jones-Evans and Westhead, 1996; Reid and Garnsey, 1997). As the EU recognised the contribution of SMEs to the economy they put policies in place to provide extra funding and resources for these firms, the European commission also presented its new policy for SMEs including new definitions and categories classification in January 2005 as illustrated in table 4.1. SMEs are small to medium enterprises categorized as micro, small and medium enterprises and includes all such enterprises as defined by the European Union regardless of legal status. To qualify as an SME a firm has to be considered an enterprise which is defined as "any entity engaged in an economic activity" SME owners determine whether they are a micro, small or medium sized enterprise by the following criteria. SMEs are usually independent and free from outside control. Characteristics of SMEs are of relatively flat organizational structure without a hierarchy and if there are employees then a more participative culture is evident. Small enterprises are defined as having fewer than 50 employees, micro having fewer than 10 and to qualify as a medium sized firm there must be fewer than 250 employees (OECD 2010)

.

Firm size is measured by employee size and balance sheet figures however due to the fact that small firms not in the public domain do not publish annual reports and may be unwilling to disclose their financial position this study has used the number of employees to gauge the size of the firm. Table 4.1 presents data for share of enterprises, employment and turnover by size of enterprise UK private sector (Start) 2008 Source Hughes and Mina (2008). The data shows that there are more small firms than larger firms involved directly in innovative activities

Table 4.1 Firm size by employee numbers

	Small	Medium	Large
Enterprise	99.3%	0.6%	0.1%
Employment	47.9%	11.5%	40.6%
Turnover	36.5%	13.6%	49.9%

Source compiled from OECD (2010)

4.4.1 Defining small high tech (or technology-based) firms

Despite lagging behind in some industries the UK high tech sector have become more proactive and is acknowledge as being leaders in research and development. (OECD 2010) This has been assisted by the government's policy of investment in science or technology parks which specialize in supporting organic R&D businesses in a range of scientific and technology areas.

According to Jones-Evans and Westhead (1996 pp 16) the increase in small high technology firms came from what they call the "flexible specialization theory" explaining the phenomena of high tech high growth firms development during recession periods as being an interaction of "demand side, supply side and policy factors".

Firms whose processes or products require a high degree of scientific or technological knowledge are often grouped as high tech firms (Rhyne et al, 1997). They usually invest in R&D and employ technically qualified personnel. Therefore these two measures are used for the purpose of this study. Firms who chose to compete in this area face rapid changes and short product life cycles and the OECD (2010) gives classification of the high tech sector to include the following industries which have been adopted globally. For the purpose of this book small high tech firms are defined by combining the characteristics of the small SME and the high tech firms described above.

4.4.2 Technology and incubation sites

The location of high tech firms is considered by many to be an important strategic factor, many small high tech firms choose to locate initially where resources and support are available by either public or private provision.

There are currently over 120 (UKBI 2009) incubator sites located in the UK some on science and technology parks others are stand-alone while further sites are linked to universities who have strong research expertise in technological development or scientific research and development.

Business incubator sites are designed to accelerate the successful development of entrepreneurial companies. They offer business support and services together with access to resources that start-ups may not be able to access through either financial constraints or necessary housing. Support is offered through the incubator management in both the incubation environment and through networking. Incubator sites although they may be located on technology parks are different due to their dedication to start-up businesses. Science and Technology parks tend to be linked to university or government sponsorship and tend to house larger projects including co - operations between large private sector firms and either government or university projects. Some incubation environments operate with a combination of both virtual and physical provision. Start up for technology firms has been assisted by the growth in incubator sites located either on existing science and technology parks or on specialist sites were clusters are encouraged to offer support for each other.

Few business parks offer business support this is the domain of incubator management and differs from them by targeting only start-ups and offering entrepreneurial support. The benefits of incubation sites is that they can stimulate enterprise and nurture innovation, however there are pitfalls when they are weaned off this support and it is how businesses employ strategies to increase their cooperation with others to maintain these networks and support systems that forms the basis for this research. The time spent in an incubation environment can depend on the research and development cycles for example science research with extensive trials and tests may require longer than a manufacturing or service that can produce quickly and bring a product or service to market through strategic management. Through literature review the prevalence of SM in manufacturing organizations has been proven (Analoui and Karami, 2003; O'Regan et al, 2008). What remains to be established is the use of SM in high tech SMEs.

4.4.3 Defining SME variables

Firms in the high tech sector will have similarities for example use of technology, markets and customers and suppliers in common. However these firms will also have characteristics that will define them and these have been chosen as the independent variables for analysis of the firm data collected during the empirical research. The variables identified in literature are age, size, location and industrial sector. Analysing these variables will enable profiling of small SMEs in the high tech sector and testing the hypothesis.

To address research objective two questions related to firm (SME) demographics formed section two of the questionnaire. These investigated the characteristics of the SMEs themselves. Respondents are asked to supply such information as firm age, size, industrial sector and employee numbers. Further firm related questions asked about operational success and achievement of goals. As discussed both financial success and employee growth are measures of a firms effectiveness for this study as cautioned against by Gulati (1998) this study will not be using traditional accounting and financial measures such as sales growth etc to measure a firms growth. R&D expenditure has been an influential variable in a firms' ability to innovate (Shefer and Frenkel, 2005). Furthermore they say the current operation and performance of a firm reflect its past experiences and routines and that by Strategic Alliances in marketing then firms "…exploration of new market opportunities and is an indication of a firm's growth orientation".

Hypothesis two is associated with finding correlation between firm demographics and strategic alliance success, information included age, size, location and industrial sector. Age is expected to be correlated with firm growth and sustainability. Figure 4.2 presents an example where strategic alliance success is a dependant variable affected by the independent variable of firm demographics. These variables are used to test hypothesis two. These view the effect that firm demographics i.e. age, size, location, industrial sector and firm activities have on alliance success. These variables have been used successfully by prior researchers as it is supported that these characteristics heavily influence the firms performance for example see (Smallbone et al 1995: Jones-Evans and Westhead 1996: Smith 2003: Garengo and Bititci 2007: Lau et al 2007: Chen and Karami 2010)

Figure 4.2 Independent and dependant variables used to test hypothesis two

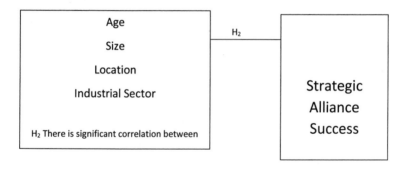

Independent Variables   **Dependant Variable**

4.5 Defining strategic management

According to Johnson and Scholes, (2008) and Byars, (1987) strategy is the direction and scope of an organisation over the long term. Through the process of Strategic Management (SM) in decision making and implementing the strategies, advantages can be gained for organizations in both markets and stakeholder expectations. SMEs have to plan for growth resulting in debate in literature regarding suitability of existing models versus creating new models to suit the entrepreneurial spirit of these organic businesses (French, 2004; French, 2009). Arguments similar to this emerge despite corroboration for the importance of SM because many micro businesses claim not to have a strategy. It is argued by some that SMEs and in particular micro firms depend on bespoke advertising, networking and building relationships (Egan, 2008) which I purport are strategies and need managing.

As literature continues to search for a paradigm that can envelope SM in all its ambiguity research will continue to focus on the application rather than on the methods used. Stonehouse & Pemberton (2002) argue that it is important that there is a distinction between strategic thinking, planning and execution and while Mintzberg advocates flexibility, it is important to plan not only where the business is going but how it will cope with environmental uncertainty. Business tools such as PESTLEC, SWOTSs and Porters Five Forces are amongst the plethora of business assistance available however SMEs according to prior literature view them as the domain of larger firms and do not employ them as readily as they could.

The significance of management as practice has been widely documented and many have strived to define it for example Olum (2004 pp. 2) "Management is the art or science of achieving goals through people", further more managers have a number of functions: Planning Controlling Organising Leading. All these are pertinent to the firm's internal environment but the manager also has to regard his external environment.

4.5.1 Planning

When managers plan they are actively choosing objectives of the business and finding the means and resources to achieve them. Decision making is involved in this process and the ability to consider options is what sets managers apart.

4.5.2 Strategic management

Strategic management has been the source of research by academics for decades. The link between environmental occurrences and firms performance was a phenomena which merited this attention and when managers discovered that by investigating certain elements in their external environment they could impact on the firms performance. The significant benefits to the firms for carrying out environmental analysis were quickly understood by top managers and these tools were used to forecast and anticipate future problems and for a firm to employ their internal capabilities and resources to place the firm in a strategic position better than their competitors.

From literature it is seen that managers of businesses will plan and operate their businesses using different strategies however it is understood that each strategic management process has three key areas i.e. strategic analysis, strategic choice and subsequently the implication of the strategy. This process would result in the firm having organisational objectives which would be disseminated across the firm. It is well documented in literature see for example (Smallbone et al, 1995, Porter, 1996) that proper strategic planning does contribute towards increased firm performance and success. It is argued that those firms who do have formalised plans in place including mission statements and business plans will perform better than those who have either ineffective plans which are not implemented in time or have no planning at all conversely entrepreneurs who are thought to be innovative and successful are considered not in need of planning (Schumpeter 1937), meanwhile Mintberg argues that having formal plans for small firms removes their ability to be flexible. There are a number of ways in research to measure a firms success or growth and these include financial factors such as sales, profits and for larger firms such items as earnings per share etc. Employee numbers especially when there is an increase are considered indicators of a firms growth and can often be considered a better measurement as some firms will reinvest profits.

Management literature has failed to explore whether firms adopt formal management strategies because of or in spite of the economic environment. Managers are classified as formal or informal planners and there is much argument about which is the best approach. From this it is seen that a strategic management approach however defined or undertaken does contribute towards a firms' performance.

4. 6 Models of strategic management

In the literature review a number of models for strategic management are included in journal papers these models have similar concepts and offer techniques for planning and have been used successfully by larger firms with smaller firms and researchers trying to adapt them to fit the purpose. Based on these the models of existing strategic management available in literature this study presents the hypothesised model of management strategy resulting in alliance formation in figure 4.5, the model suggests the interdependence of behaviour and practice in the quest for improved firm performance. Table 4.3 illustrates an example of the processes involved when managers assess their environments.

4.7 Chapter summary

This chapter has discussed the use of conceptual frameworks to link theory with the research questions to identify variables and models that can be used to illustrate the way the concepts are created.

The key themes as discussed in chapters one, two and three have been reviewed to produce a framework for analysing managers, SMEs, strategic management and alliance behaviour.

Contemporary research has identified relationships between management and firm performance. This research suggests a direct relationship between:

"management and firm demographics and successful strategic alliances resulting in improved firm performance"

Chapter five presents the research methodology in which the variables will be utilised to construct the questionnaire and to determine data collection methods and analysis.

Chapter Five: Research Methodology

5.1 Introduction

This chapter illustrates the process that is required to carry out this research. There are a number of steps necessary to carry out in order to complete the research (Saunders et al, 2007; Easterby-Smith et al, 2010). Both these suggest that the research process is not necessarily rational and straightforward but may require rethinking and revisiting steps when objectives cannot be met. When a step is re visited it then impinges on the whole process and may need reworking of subsequent steps Easterby-Smith et al, (2010).

5.1.1 Presentation of theoretical knowledge of methodologies

Methodologies are simply the system of organising and structuring theoretical and practical activity. Methodologies in the social sciences are many and varied and will depend on the interests of the researcher and the resources available to them. For example (Hoskisson et al, 1999; Hair et al, 2007).

Therefore presentation of theoretical knowledge of methodologies simply means looking at the previous theories and presenting them in a way that guides the reader to what has previously been established as theory in a particular field and how their own ideas may be guided by or contribute to expand or corroborate existing theories. The presentation of these theories can take place within the literature review or during the process of creating a conceptual framework. Theoretical knowledge helps translate current information about a topic into practical knowledge so enables us to carry out our own research into the subject. There is a link between prior theories and methods that you decide to use in your own research. Hair et al (2007 pp 37)

"Theories provide key inputs into the research process".

For example if previous researchers into management behaviour return good results from surveys then future research is likely to show similar qualities if that type of research is carried out. Furthermore, the method used for data collection and interpretation is likely to impact on the theory drawn from the results. In business research historically research and frameworks were centred on larger firms (Das and He, 2006) more recently there has been a rise in research and theoretical frameworks based on SME research and in particular strategic management and strategic alliances (Ju et al, 2005; Hair et al, 2007; Saxena and Bharadwaj, 2009; Das and Kumar, 2010). These examples range from prescriptive material for practitioners to theories developed through empirical research.

5.2 Aims and objectives of the study

The aim of the study is to investigate the strategic alliance success in SMEs in the UK. To achieve this research questions are related to:

- Management demographics
- Firm demographics
- Strategic alliances

The research question, objectives and hypothesis are presented below together with detailed propositions.

Research Question   How do management and firm demographics affect strategic alliance success in the high tech sector?

Proposition 1 Identify key demographics of owner managers including gender, age, education and managerial experience to establish the affect that these demographics and background characteristics have on alliance success.

Research objectives and hypothesis

Research objective 1 - To investigate the relationship between demographics and background characteristics of managers and strategic alliance success.

Hypothesis 1 - H_1 There is significant correlation between demographics and background characteristics of managers and strategic alliance success.

Research objective 2 - To investigate the relationship between demographics and background characteristics of firms and strategic alliances.

Hypothesis 2 - H_2 There is significant correlation between firm's demographics and background characteristics and successful strategic alliances

5.3 Research methods and strategy

5.3.1 The process of research

Deciding on the process of research will depend on what the research questions are and the methods used. Generally, the research process describes what type of data will be collected, where the data will be collected and period for data collection; it will also describe the target population and the rational for choosing that sample from the available population. Furthermore as illustrated in figure 5.1 it will describe the order in which each step will be taken.

Figure 5.1 Research process

Identify Need for Research

Decide on a research topic

Source
adapted

from   Review the literature

Decide on a research philosophy and approach

Develop research design

Collect Data

Analyse the data

Discuss the results and make recommendations
for future research

Saunders et al (2007, p10)

123

Management research is considered distinct from other forms of research in the social sciences for example Easterby –Smith et al (2008 pp 11) states that

> "management research has unusual features which make it
>
> distinctive both in form and content, especially in comparison
>
> with other social science disciplines"

Further, more according to Saunders et al (2007) it is important to choose the correct research method. To do this it is necessary to understand the philosophies and principles of social science and in particular management research. Examples of research method include surveys which can include self-reporting questionnaires (Sanyal and Guvenli, 2004; Ju et al, 2005; Meehan and Muir, 2008; Chen and Karami, 2010), Interviews (Pidduck, 2006) Case studies (Saxena and Bharadwaj, 2009) group discussions (Reynolds and Lancaster, 2007). Others have carried out qualitative research using secondary data to present and contrast existing theories, frameworks and research for example see Hoskisson et al, (1999) to produce review papers and others have used a mixture of these (Pidduck, 2006). Research into strategy and in particular strategic alliances has resulted in a mess of contradictions, models and paradigms without offering any way out of the confusing arena of strategic alliance criteria and selection. However, Gartner (2010) suggests it is possible to wade through this mess and emerge with some new and concise ideas, while Das and Kumar (2010) strive to make sense of inter-partner strategic alliances.

5.3.2 Research Philosophy

According to Saunders et al (2007) when undertaking research the aim is to create new knowledge and to do this there has to be an understanding of which philosophical stance is being taken as this gives the reader access to assumptions that the researcher has made about what is occurring and what their interest in that phenomena is. Our values are an integral part of our philosophy and literature suggests that if we have a set of assumptions about phenomena and how we should carry out our studies and place significant reliance on our data then we are likely to think of our research philosophy as epistemology.

These stances will have an impact on the research strategy and design therefore making a decision about the stance requires careful consideration. Having examined the extant literature on social science research and in particular management research two traditional views on undertaking research. It is the view of some for example Easterby-Smith (2008) and Saunders et al (2007) that the two contrasting views of positivism and social constructivism can be combined and used in a pragmatic way.

Those who adopt a positivist stance for example (Shefer and Frenkel, 2005; Grawe et al, 2009; Chen and Karami, 2010) will develop a research strategy and look for hard evidence and chose to carry out empirical research collecting data to test hypothesis. They chose to look for patterns in the data and observe how frequently the same phenomena or answer is given. The positivist researcher is removed from the research object and remains independent. On the other hand, those who adopt a social constructionism stance look for interpretation and view reality as something that is not objective and countable but something that comes from within and relies on intuition. The researcher is not removed and views human interests as part of the science. While positivists strive to explain why certain phenomena occur the social constructionist will obtain a general understanding of the situation and gather data that can result in ideas being generated (Hughes and Beasley, 2008).

Social constructionists observe holistically an environment or situation while the positivist finds a small part to investigate for example they do not look at an organisation but take the manager or culture or possibly employees and investigate the causality of the action of one of these on the others or another phenomena. For the same reason social constructionists chose small sample numbers to investigate completely while the positivist will search for large numbers often selected randomly from a population.

With regard to the above discussion, I have chosen to adopt a pragmatic stance and while the over-reaching philosophy for this study will be positivism when considering the interaction of managers with their internal and external environments social constructivism will be considered as a contributor to the interpretations.

5.4 Research approach

Having chosen to conduct the research from a positivist stance it is necessary to adopt a research approach that complements it. In social science research deductive and inductive approaches are considered appropriate. Inductive approaches are more often related to interpretivism using secondary data or previous theories and thereby social constructivism for example see (Rogers, 2001; Mellat-Parast and Digman, 2007). The researcher collects data and after analysis suggests a theory to explain what has happened or what is happening (Berry and Taggart, 1996; Shefer and Frenkel, 2005).

On the other hand according to Saunders et al (2007) deductive approaches are associated to positivism as the researcher will know the existing theory or develop their own theory and hypothesis. While developing this theory the researcher remains independent however it can be argued that as they choose the questions to answer and to some extent the participants' then impartiality is not guaranteed. They will then develop a research strategy to enable testing of the hypothesis, as with the positivist philosophy the results have to be measured and generalised across populations. Despite the differences of these two approaches like other management research options in research do not have to be either or they can be combined to give robustness and strength to the research.

This study is a combination of deductive and inductive since the objectives of the research was not to test existing theory but to understand management characteristics that influence management decision making about engagement in strategic alliances. To do this it is necessary to understand the existing theories and using inductive methods enables the use of grounded theory to assist in building the conceptual framework illustrated in chapter four. It is understood that due to the time constraints that the study will be cross-sectional.

5.4.1 Qualitative or quantitative data collection

In deciding to use qualitative research the researcher is relying on constructing meaning from only words that he is given on the other hand quantitative research allows the collection of hard evidence in the pooled frequency that respondents have indicated the same answer or choice. Qualitative data can come from sources other than the respondent for example financial reports while data is collected during quantitative data collection in order to test theory. The benefits of using quantitative methods are that putting all the data into simple numerical form enables data to be easily compared. The analysis is statistical and does not allow for subjective interpretations therefore the validity of the data can be easily assessed.

A drawback of quantitative data is that it misses out on elements of personality and feelings of the participants. Hard data enables coding to be carried out so that statistical analysis can be carried out this prevents the necessity of theorising about the data collected as happens in qualitative data collection. As sample sizes can be controlled with a larger population response enabled in quantitative data collection then general reliability of the data can be assumed. As researchers when we are presenting information that may cause a reaction from people or will result in managers making important business decisions it is important that the information is based on hard evidence and this advice (Easterby-Smith et al, 2010) is heeded. Many researchers use existing theory to develop their own research questions and then carry out empirical research to provide the evidence (Smallbone et al, 1995; Berry, 1996; March and Gunasekaran, 1999; Saffu and Mamman, 1999; Kathuria and Porth, 2003; Ju et al, 2005; Shefer and Frenkel, 2005; Pidduck, 2006; Jaouen and Gundolf, 2009; Chen and Karami, 2010).

5.5 Research strategy

The literature that offers assistance and guides to carrying out management research offers two main methods of collecting data using surveys. These are surveys and interviews and within these two areas there are options for postal surveys, face to face, electronic mailings, face to face interview, telephone interviews however neither are purported to be most appropriate and the decision on which method to choose depends on the researcher using items such as deadlines, cost, quantity of data required or perhaps what the researcher intends to do with the data collected. For example if they intend to test hypothesise then quantitative data collected via survey might be most appropriate.

According to (Berry and Taggart, 1998; Karami, 2010 pp 115;; Simsek et al, 2010), postal surveys are a good method of collecting data "because of its geographical reach". Respondents who are widely dispersed are reached quickly and for less cost than travel to interviews. Respondents can take their time to consider the questions however as already discussed there is the danger of a low response rate. The low response rate can be because of the questionnaire design, lack of interest in the topic by the respondent and also the familiarity of the manager with doctoral research and its importance to the student. Freepost self-addressed envelopes were also included to encourage the return of the questionnaire, the key advantages and disadvantages are presented in table 5.1.

Table 5.1 Example of advantages and disadvantages of postal questionnaires

Advantages	Disadvantages
Cost per respondent is low compared with face to face interviews	Low response rates
Beneficial when respondents are widely dispersed	Have no control over who actually completes the questionnaire
Increases the accuracy of the answers given, during an interview the respondent might be reluctant to speak the truth	The respondent might misunderstand a question
A respondent can check details for example how many employees which they may not recall during an interview	Questions are avoided which lead to missing data.
A respondent may feel they have anonymity when responding to a postal questionnaire.	

Source adapted from Easterby-Smith et al (2010)

As the research required the collection of quantitative data for hypothesis testing and the population sample was high it was felt that a postal questionnaire might yield the best response given the time element (Saunders et al 2007: Easterby-Smith et al 2010: Karami 2010).

A postal questionnaire that was self-administered was chosen form for data collection as this is recognised as an appropriate way to conduct social science research and in particular management research. This method has advantages and disadvantages. For the purpose of this study the advantages were exploited and the disadvantages were avoided. To do this the questionnaire was used as the main research instrument and through postal delivery.

5.5.1 Constructing the questionnaire

Using guidance from prior research into appropriate demographic data requirements, management data requirements and strategic alliance data questions and methodologies from (Berry and Taggart, 1998; March and Gunasekaran, 1999; Ju et al, 2005; Shefer and Frenkel, 2005; Simsek et al, 2010) are replicated in this study. The required information was compiled based on the research questions and the conceptual framework presented in chapter four.

1   Management demographic Information
     Age
     Gender
     Education
     Managerial experience
     Management perceptions

2   SME demographic Information
     Age of firm
     Size of firm
     Focus of the firm
     Strategic management of the firm
     Organisation achievement of goals and objectives
     Core capabilities

A closed question occurs where the respondent is directed to choose an answer from a list of possible answers. For example, question 2.5 asks which of the following do you prefer to be focused on?

O   Your local market

O   A broader market

O   Selling at a lower price than your competitor does

O   Having a product that is different to your competitor

An open-ended question occurs when the respondent gives an answer of their choice. For example, question 2.11 asks What were the company's sales in the past year? This requires the respondent to enter a monetary value in a text box.

There are advantages and disadvantages to both of these options and offering a category of "other" can limit these.

5.5.2 Structuring the questionnaire

The first step in the construction of the questionnaire was to decide the data that would be required to answer the research questions and test the hypothesis. Broadly using the research model employed by Dvir et al (2010) to divide the questionnaire into sections that would enable grouping the variables.

Managerial Demographics including background characteristics

Firm demographics

Strategic management behaviour

Alliance behaviour

- Questions 1.1 to 1.5 asked for personal details about the participant. It was aimed at creating a profile of the managers the use of which would be replicated in the following chapters. Variables considered that influence strategic alliance formations are related to gender, age, educational attainment and managerial experience. These were closed ended questions asking the respondents to choose from a number of responses.

- Questions 2.1 to 2.15 were designed to build a profile of the firms and the industrial sectors they were in. The questions included location, investment and sales, firm performance and the products it had in its pipeline. The questions in this section were closed and opened and also firm's performance was ranked on a four point likert scale from excellent to not applicable. Questions were also asked to determine the sector that the firms were in.

- The third section asked questions 3.1 to 3.15 about the alliance activities of the participant firms. It sought information about the critical success factors perceived by the managers. These factors have been widely researched during the last decade by others for example see Chen and Karami 2010, Vyas et al 1995 Questions in this section were both closed answer questions and those were ranking was used on a five point likert scale ranging from very important to not important. Managers were also asked to indicate their motivations for engaging in alliances and also to consider the areas that might contribute to failure of an alliance.

5.5.2.1 Strategic management

This section combines the answers from 2.15 with all previous sections to obtain information about the firm's strategic management practices. This will inform the study about the managers motivations, alliances experiences, partnering, decision making, strategic management and critical success factors considered for strategic alliances.

5.5.2.2 Performance

The managers were asked to indicate how well they considered the technical objectives of the firm were being met, They were asked to use a five point likert scale ranging from very important to not important to indicate how well they considered the importance of the objectives being met on schedule, not met on schedule or whether there was outstanding achievement of the technical objectives.

5.5.2.3 Performance indicators

The uses of traditional methods of measuring success for firms such as financial performance were not considered appropriate for this questionnaire. Prior research for example Smallbone et al (1995) have excluded growth from PIs as they felt that SMEs did not necessarily grow and Lunnan and Haugland (2008) cite information from prior research where the financial aspect and performance relate to the parent firms and not to the actual alliance. The disadvantages of using them are displayed in table 5.2.

The rational for excluding financial measures as PIs include:

- Young companies may be entrenched in research and development and may not yet began to commercialise their products and would therefore not have significant financial assets, however the respondents were asked to indicate if they had attracted any investment, reinvested themselves and also to indicate their sales. It was considered that sales might be exaggerated as with the launch of a new product, sales are very rapid and these figures may not give a good indication as there may not yet be any followers in the market and the firm is enjoying the whole of the market share.

- These firms are not in the public domain and therefore their finances are not publically available.

- Assets in particular knowledge are not easily measured and therefore even when data is obtained it can be inaccurate.

For these reasons operational success is analysed and where supplied financial data is subjected to descriptive statistics.

For example a firm who is heavily involved in R&D, patent applications and registration these can be considered measures of performance. This however takes into consideration the time to obtain a patent and often firms have lengthy trial periods. For some sectors patents are not considered important while for others they are considered important and may be requested prior to completion of the research. Further more many will wish to keep their products secret and will therefore not seek patents.

Question 2.12 also considers the ability of the firm to attract first class scientists as a measure of the firm's performance. Questions such as these enable the study to evaluate and create a profile of what is considered important by the manager as a contribution to firm performance and success. Other research used multiple Performance Indicators (PIs) to measure growth while this study only used growth in employment. Some studies have found no significant relationship between SM and performance as a result of the PIs used. Empirical work by Garengo and Bititci (2007) found that management style impacted on the type of performance measures used by SMEs, while Richard et al (2009) researched the best methods for measuring organisational performance concluding that there is no one best method and that the researching of performance measures requires more triangulation and longitudinal studies. A study by Dobbs and Hamilton (2007) reviewed the prior research into business growth and indicated that more researchers used employment and sales as an indicator of firm performance than any other type of performance measure.

Respondents are asked to indicate their gender, age and educational qualifications together with their managerial experience. Manager's gender is required to ensure no bias is because of gender. Age and risk adversity are often related therefore a managers age is considered an important variable. The educational qualifications are the highest-level qualification that the manager has. The categories are coded with 1 for the lower level qualifications and 6 for doctoral degree. To accommodate any other specific qualifications the category other is also offered. Managerial experience measures the number of years a manager has worked in management throughout their career. Another variable is offered to indicate whether or not they own the business to find a relationship between ownership and management.

5.6 Pilot study

As the information used to construct the questionnaire came from academic theory and research it was necessary to test whether or not these questions would be equally applicable and understood by practitioners. Prior to the completion of the questionnaire the supervisor had provided advice about questionnaire construction and revisions were made despite this rigour it was necessary to also test this questionnaire on managers from the intended population. Responses from these managers would ensure the validity of the questionnaire and its user friendliness for the proposed respondents. The pilot was conducted on line with members of ISBE being the target sample, the responses then enabled a final review of the questionnaire prior to distribution. There were only 25 responses received and these were not confirmed as high tech firms however, these responses highlighted areas where the questions could be reworded as many questions were left unanswered due to their ambiguity. Thus these were reformatted to make them user friendly.

5.6.1.Source of data and sampling

The target population was owner managed SMEs in the high tech sector in the United Kingdom. This population was chosen as prior historical research have focused on the larger firms (Smith, 2003) and given the importance of the SME to the economy following prior more contemporary researchers (Ju et al, 2005) and surveying the SME manager To avoid the possibility of receiving responses from public or large companies in the public domain the sample was taken from the companies house directory which lists all companies limited by guarantee. Due to the large number of registered companies, firms were selected using SIC codes relating to manufacturing as this is the domain of high tech firms and then the firms were narrowed down to younger SMEs and who were clearly not partnerships. Five thousand firms were selected and were sent the survey via the Royal Mail.

The firm type that was required for this survey have similar characteristics and are usually found on science or technology parks with a few situated in incubator sites and a few based on their own but within proximity of support services.

Over a period of six weeks a database with five thousand SMEs was collated, one disadvantage to this method was that individual manager's names were not obtained. Firms were chosen by SIC code and identification of being considered high tech as defined by the OECD. Those firms that it thought were associated with larger firms and considered multi national were excluded, as they did not adhere to the criteria for selecting firms. Having engaged with alliances was not a criterion for the firm being asked to participate as I was also interested in the motivations of firms who avoided alliances.

5.6.1.1 Sample selection

As SMEs are not always registered for VAT or PAYE purposes it is not always easy to determine the existence of firms. Using this method to obtain the sample was considered most appropriate. As discussed research is not limited to one industry sector but taking from a range that includes, nano-technology, biotechnology, telecommunications, software development, chemical, petrochemical, bio medical and other technology sectors. This enables the observation of the dynamics of a range of industry types who will react and choose alliance partners differently (Lin et al, 2009). This is partially because some are labour or capital intensive while others are technology intensive and as a result what they seek and what they have to offer will vary as will the managerial types to be found in these industries. Research highlights that response rates for mailed surveys can be low, however it is anticipated that due to the large volume of potential participants that there will be a significant number of respondents.

5.6.5 Rationale for choosing SMEs

SMEs have characteristics that separate them from MNEs and therefore researching them will enable gaps in knowledge to be filled. The following are rational for choosing SMEs.

- If registered as Ltd there was an expectation that there would not be multiple stakeholders intervening as found in many MNEs and therefore the owner manager would be responsible for all decision making.
- SME managers are usually the owners and would therefore have both an economic and emotional investment in the business.
- Historically SMEs use networking and internal resources to fund growth strategies.

5.6.6 The process of the survey

As the management literature directly relating to perceptions and motivations in SMEs is limited the survey was aimed at this population to collect data to bridge the gap. To do this it was attempted to collect data from a sample of 5,000 managers of SMEs that are limited companies in the UK using multi stage sampling technique, firstly putting firms into categorise that I was interested in and then randomly picked my 5000 from the sample. The manager who was also likely to be the owner was considered to be best placed to providing not only his own demographic data but also the data on the firm's demographics and organisational performance and strategy as it is assumed he would be the person controlling this.

The questionnaires were sent accompanied by a covering letter explaining the importance of the survey in understanding management behaviour in SMEs. Manages were assured of anonymity as all data would be aggregated and requested to complete the questionnaire in order for sufficient data to be collected and all participants were offered a summary of the results as way of acknowledging their contribution to the research. In order that no participant would incur costs and to minimize response bias a stamped addressed envelope was also included with the questionnaire. A number were returned by the royal mail as undeliverable while others were sent by the respondent as unwilling or unable to participate these are discussed later.

5.6.7 Non-response

As mentioned the disadvantages of conducting postal questionnaire surveys can be limited by employing some measures. The following measures were employed to improve the respondent rate.

- A covering letter was attached to the questionnaire. This served the purpose of explaining the research and highlighting the importance of the research to the respondents. The authors full contact details were supplied to encourage respondents to contact the researcher if they had any questions about the questionnaire or indeed about the research in general.

- The covering letter assured anonymity and explained that the responses would be aggregated. A freepost envelope was also included to enable the return of the questionnaire, it was anticipated that this would increase the response rate.

- The respondents were also asked if they would like a summary of the report when complete it was anticipated that this would increase the response rate.

5.7 Non-response bias

As postal survey responses are reported to be low compared to some other methods, it was important to test for non-response bias. It is argued by some that the responses received late would be similar to those who do not respond at all. To test for this Mann-Whitney tests were run between the first 50 and the last 50 responses, using the categorical variable with two groups i.e.

gender and a continuous variable regarding motivation to seek alliances. As can be seen in figure 5.3for these variables the z value is -1.20 with a significant level of p=.263. As the probability value is larger than .05 the result is not significant. There is no statistical difference in the response scores of those who completed the questionnaire early and those that returned it after a longer length of time.

Table 5.3 Results of the Mann-Whitney U Test

	What might motivate your firm to seek alliances?
Mann-Whitney U	521.000
Wilcoxon W	2666.000
Z	-1.120
Asymp. Sig. (2-tailed)	.263

Source Research Data   Grouping Variable: - Gender

On receipt of returned questionnaires via the royal mail it was necessary to code each one to enable them to be put into SPSS to aid analysis. As discussed in chapter four the production of the coding directory enabled data to be inputted into SPSS using its variable value. To recap the directory included a variable name that would be acceptable for SPSS, a variable label and a variable value were also included. The data entry view of SPSS was used to create the spreadsheet and then data view was used to input the data.

5.8 Data entry and the process of data analysis

As previously discussed the data needed to undergo preliminary analysis, data was presented in graphic form such as pie charts, bar graphs in preparation for hypothesis testing. This preliminary analysis enabled testing of the validity of the data and how dispersed it was using means and standard deviation.

Once the data was entered into SPSS frequency tests were run to ensure that there were not detrimental amounts of data missing. As anticipated the participants had opted for not answering some questions. This can be done for a number of reasons, assumption that it does not apply to them, did not understand the questions and felt that the question was too intrusive. For many of the questions not answering would not bias the responses as the survey was to test perceptions of the managers. Despite this the responses where the participant did not answer questions relating to their demographics and therefore independent variables were removed. Using this procedure did reduce the total number of respondents however, there was confidence that the remaining data was valid, in chapter 6 Cronbach Alpha results confirm this.

5.8.1 Use of statistical measures

As the data collected displays areas of abnormality i.e. do not have a uniform distribution it is assumed that parametric testing may not be most appropriate measure of the survey data, as they do not confirm to requirements for parametric testing Pellant (2001) therefore for this research non parametric tests which are more forgiving than parametric tests about abnormal distribution and also they respond well to data measured in ordinal scales therefore for this research non parametric tests have been utilised. To carry out investigation into the relationships between variables

143

Spearman rank order correlation for non-categorical data was utilised. This was used as the distribution of the collected data was not uniform. As illustrated above in table 5.3 Mann-Whitney U test was used to testing for differences e.g. between response and non-responses.

5.8.2 Outline of data analysis

The data obtained from the postal survey was measured on nominal and ordinal scales and therefore parametric testing would normally be excluded, however ranked data has been successfully tested using regression analysis and Pallant (2001) suggests that it has been successfully applied to other research then they can be employed with the analysis being aware that there may be discrepancies and using it as a support for other findings rather than a purveyor of the truth.

Descriptive analysis is undertaken to produce the profiles of managers, the firm and alliance activity. It also identifies primary motives for manager's engagement or avoidance with strategic alliances. Mean scores of each factor are calculated together with standard deviation and percentages where applicable.

Rank Spearman's correlation coefficient was employed to analyse the relationship between managers and firms characteristics and motivations for strategic alliances.

Independent t tests were undertaken to conduct mean difference analysis in the variables related to critical success factors perceived by managers. The statistical methods and the authors who have used this methodology are illustrated in table 5.4.

Table 5.4 The statistical methods employed in the data analysis

Statistical Methods	Area Applied	Authors
Cronbach Alpha	Management	Tovstiga and Tulugurova (2007) Fening et al (2008)
Mann U Whitney	For testing non response bias	Pellant (2001)
Descriptive analysis	A profile of the respondents and surveyed firms. The primary motives for engaging in or avoidance of strategic alliances. The importance of critical success factors	Chen & Karami (2010)
Rank Spearman Correlation analysis	Association between managerial characteristics, firm's characteristics and the primary motivations for strategic alliances.	Simsek et al (2010)
Independent samples t test	Mean difference in assessment of critical success factors between experienced firms and inexperienced firms. Test differences between response and non responses	Simsek et al (2010)

Source Multiple Sources

5.8.3 Responses from samples

Figure 5.3 shows the numbers of responses received and the category they fall into. The large number returned by the post office was unexpected due to the fact that the database was considered up to date. This result shows how quickly firms can become liquidated, sold or acquired by the competition.

Figure 5.3 Response tally

5000 Questionnaires distributed	
Returned Questionnaires	**Other Responses**
528 Completed Questionnaires 444 Usable 84 Unusable This provides a usable response of 8.88%	14 letters sent with questionnaire with encouragement and offering further information if required. 21 Letters explaining why they could not take part 138 returned by post office
Overall response rate 11.26%	

Source Research Data

Typical response rates for studies addressing strategic issues are 10–12% (O'Regan and Sims, 2008) for management 14% (Simsek et al, 2010) therefore despite the relatively small number of respondents the results are considered satisfactory.

5.9 Ethical considerations

According to Saunders et al (2007 p 178) "In the context of research, ethics refers to the appropriateness of your behaviour in relation to the rights of those who become the subject of your work". For this reason an ethical stance was taken to construct the research strategy and choosing participants.

To ensure the privacy of the prospective participants individual manages names were not stored which meant that responses were kept anonymous and confidential. The individuals were free to accept or decline the opportunity to take part in the survey this voluntary involvement meant that there was not any pressure on people to participate. This was further ensured by not offering any enticements to participate, the only gesture towards ensuring the postal participants returned theirs was to enclose a SAE and this was done to ensure that the respondents did not incur any costs by participating.

5.10 Chapter summary

This chapter has discussed the philosophical stance of the author and the research methodology chosen. Based on the research proposition, research questions and hypotheses proposed in chapters 1 and 4 this chapter has presented the research method used for this study after reviewing the options available. The methods chosen were assumed to be most appropriate for meeting the objectives of the study. A deductive approach has been adopted and employs a cross sectional research method. The unit of analysis is the manager of SME high tech firms. A postal questionnaire has been chosen as the instrument for collecting data. The questionnaire design is such that the benefits of postal surveys are exploited. To further ensure the reliability of the data steps have been taken to minimise error.

Using qualitative descriptive analysis supported by statistical analysis was found to be appropriate in that management research requires the presentation of in depth data, which is accessible for practitioners therefore by profiling the answers the data, is easily accessible while the statistical data provides further analysis for the academic audience. Using SPSS to analyse the data enabled the exploration of the data and identified that some of the data collected violated some rules of analysis and therefore appropriate means of data testing were found.

The questionnaire is split into three sections with the first being related to demographic information about the respondent i.e. the manager of the SME. Section two collects data about the firm including size and age. Section three is composed of questions about the strategic alliance engagement and management.

The sample firms are taken from high tech firms identified through OECD and EU definition and SIC codes (SIC 2007). From the returned questionnaires 444 did not have vital information missing so were identified as valid. Validity of the responses were ensured by Cronbach Alpha test and Mann U Whitney tests which were performed to ensure that non response bias did not have significant effect on the results. Appropriate statistical analysis tests were identified together with means for displaying the information. In chapter six the descriptive data analysis is presented and statistical data analysis is presented in chapter seven with a synthesis of the findings with literature presented in chapter eight.

Chapter six: Descriptive Data Analysis

6.1 Introduction

The methodology for data collection was discussed fully in chapter five. This chapter discusses the data analysis process including testing the reliability of the data collected. The data collection method was a self completing questionnaire delivered by post targeting SMEs in the high tech industries. Five Thousand companies were chosen and I used multi stage sampling technique, firstly putting firms into categorise that I was interested in and then randomly picked 5000 from the sample using the sic codes as defined by the OECD. This chapter reviews the data collected and analysis the findings to address the research propositions discussed in chapter one and in the conceptual framework chapter i.e. chapter four.

The use of the postal survey was to obtain a sufficient sample of suitable potential participants to help address the dearth of empirical research into the decision making of SME managers regarding strategic alliance formation of SMEs in the high tech sector and thereby explore their strategic management practices.

This chapter presents the descriptive analysis of the managers, the respondent firms, the alliance behaviour of the firms and firm performance through its strategic choices. Chapter seven presents the statistical analysis of the data to establish relationships between the variables and to test the hypothesis and answer the research questions. Chapter eight will discuss the findings from chapters six and seven and provide some explanation for the results.

6.2 Reliability statistics

As discussed in Chapter one, and four the companies targeted were SMEs who were registered limited companies and who were defined by the OECD and EU through definition and SIC 2007 as being a high tech company.

The overall response rate was 11.26% and therefore reliability statistics are carried out. To test the reliability of statistics in particular where a low percentage is received it is necessary to carry out some internal tests on the data.

6.2.1 Cronbach Alpha

Many of the variables were measured on a scale similar to the Likert scale therefore it was necessary to carry out a reliability test and for this Cronbach Alpha was used. The importance of reliability testing is discussed by (Fening et al, 2008; Tovstiga & Tulugurova, 2007, O'Regan & Ghobadian, 2002). The literature provided external validity as did the pilot test for the questionnaire.

Internal consistency for the scales used in determining the use of environmental analysis has been established by using Cronbach Alpha. Previous researchers have reported a Cronbach Alpha of between .79 & .88 Tovstiga & Tulugurova (2007) 0.74 and 0.84 Fening et al (2008) this study revealed a Cronbach Alpha of 0.806 for management variables, .703 for firm variables and .730 for alliance variables therefore reliability can be assumed, the data is presented in table 6.1.

Table 6.1 Cronbach Alpha for management variables

Construct	Cronbach Alpha	No. of Items
Management variables	.806	26
Firm Variables	.703	16
Alliance Variables	.730	26

Source Research Data

6.3 Descriptive Statistics

Descriptive statistics are the basis of the quantitative data analysis. They present and describe the basic features of the data in the study, the advantages of this is detailed in table 6.2. For this study they will provide a simple summary of each of the themes under study i.e. the manager, the firm, strategic management and strategic alliances. The data is summarised and used to draw some assumptions about the studied phenomena using inferential statistics to make judgements about what is going on or what might happen. It enables similarities amongst the data to be used to profile the studied units. The analysed data is presented in graphic form and tables. The variables are presented in table form and are examined one at a time (univariate analysis) to identify the distribution, central tendency and dispersion. Cross tabulation has also been employed cited by March and Gunasekaran (1999) as being a reliable method of identifying relationships between variables.

Table 6.2 Advantages and disadvantages of descriptive statistics

Advantages	Disadvantages
Essential for arranging and displaying data Smith (2003)	Can be misused, misinterpreted, and incomplete often not subjected to robust analysis Saunders et al (2007), Easterby-Smith et al (2010)
Form the basis of rigorous data analysis Gartner (2010)	Be of limited use when samples and populations are small Simsek et al (2009)
Be much easier to work with, interpret, and discuss than raw data	Requires time for analysis and explanation
Help examine the tendencies, spread, normality, and reliability of a data set March and Gunasekaran (1999)	Fail to fully specify the extent to which non-normal data are a problem
Can be presented both graphically and numerically	Offer little information about causes and effects
Include useful techniques for summarizing data in visual form	False assumptions made if data is not analyzed completely
Form the basis for more advanced statistical methods Beverland and Bretherton (2001)	

Source compiled from multiple sources – The references contained in these tables do not only reflect the opinion of the authors but also an informed opinion on the way they have presented their data, for example Smith (2003) used tables and figures to effectively present results.

6.4 Manager demographics

Questions one to six of section one and question one from section two on the questionnaire were used to gain demographic information about the respondents i.e. managers of SMEs in the high tech sector in the UK. This data has been aggregated to produce a profile of the managers. Profiling the respondents in this manner enables the researcher to establish a model of managers operating in the high tech sector in the 21st Century. The collected data enables the researcher to draw conclusions about managers of SMEs in the high tech sector and their decision making practices and the ability to maintain firm performance. As prior experiences will affect their current behaviour this is considered important and central to the study. The companies targeted during the data collection were all limited companies and therefore the firms would not be subjected to the influence of stakeholders. Having removed this factor it is expected that the managers will not be under pressure to take risks which may result in poor firm performance. As owner managers, it is expected that the respondent's demographics will play an important factor in their decision-making, firm performance and strategic alliance success. The demographic information as discussed in chapters one and five includes age, gender, qualifications and educational attainment as well as length of time in business or experience as a manager. This information is presented in table 6.3.

Table 6.3 provides a profile of the respondents which is summarised generally below and then through graphs and tables is discussed thoroughly. The data presented includes the variables, the categories that fall under these variable headings and the frequency in which they occur in the collected data. The data is then displayed as percentages with the mean and standard deviation displayed to allow further analysis of the data.

Of the 444 usable responses the majority of the respondents were males (n=382 86%). Only 14% (n=62) of the respondents were female. In the respondent firms 31.5% of the managers are aged between 41 and 50 years old with only 1.1% being under 20. Those aged between 21 and 30 are also poorly represented with only 4.7% respondents being in this age category. Overall the highest categories are those where the respondents are between 41 and 60 years with a large percentage who were over 60. Fifty three of the firms were managed by people over 61 years of age and when carrying out statistical analysis it was noted that there is significant correlation between the age of the owner and age of the firm (p=.201**).

The majority of the respondents were educated to postgraduate level. Less than 20% of the respondents do not have a higher education qualification. Taking age into account nearly 20% of the managers has had more than 5 years managerial experience. 77.5% of the managers reported that they were the owner of the firm indicating that these managers have been involved in the firm since start up and are responsible for strategic planning and decision making. They have responsibility for all the decisions and also reap the benefit from successful firm performance. It is likely that these managers are motivated to employ practical business tools to increase firm performance and engage in strategic alliances.

The descriptive statistics illustrated in and taken from table 6.3 profile of respondents imply that managers of high tech SMEs are characterised as being two distinct groups. The first group identifies the managers as being well-educated young males holding at least an undergraduate degree and have gained some managerial experience. The second group contains older persons with significant managerial experience. The remainder of this section presents the analysis of the individual characteristics.

Table 6.3 Profile of Managers of High Tech SMEs

Variable	Category	Frequency	Percentage	Mean	S.D
Manager's Gender (N=444)	Male	382	86%		
	Female	62	14%		
Manager's Age (N=444)	<20	5	1.1%	4.4	1.18
	21-30	21	4.7%		
	31-40	70	15.8%		
	41-50	140	31.5%		
	51-60	114	25.7%		
	61+	94	21.2%		
Manager's Education Level (N=444)	O Levels	15	3.4%	4.68	1.45
	A Levels	26	5.9%		
	Diploma	30	6.8%		
	U-Degree	127	28.6%		
	Masters	102	23.%		
	PhD	105	23.6%		
	Other	39	39%		
Manager's Experience (N=438)	1-5 years	73	16.4%		
	6-10 years	60	13.5%		

	11-15 years	70	15.8%	3.48	1.52
	16-20 years	69	15.5%		
	20+ years	167	37.6%		
Founder of the firm (N=439)	Yes	344	77.5%		
	No	95	21.4%		

Source Research Data

6.4.1 Gender

Gender has been identified in literature as playing a key part in business planning and firm performance and therefore it was important that for this survey it was a key variable as it is anticipated that men and women may behave differently towards engaging in strategic alliances and therefore it was necessary to examine how gender might influence alliance activity. Question 1.1 asked participants to indicate their gender, respondents who failed to indicate their gender were removed from the study. It is expected that managers of high tech companies whether male or female would engage in strategic management. The responses are aggregated in table 6.3 and presented in figure 6.1 to show the distribution of gender. The total number of respondents who indicated their gender was 444 the majority of respondents were male (n=382, 86%) with only (n=62, 14%) being female, further analysis shows (mean = 1.14 , SD = .35. These figures are similar to those found by Karami (2007) when investigating the electronic industry confirming that men are more likely to be found in managerial positions in high tech industries, this research is corroborated by Byast and Karami (2009) where it was found that women were more prolific as managers in the service sector than men.

Figure 6.1 Pie chart to show distribution of gender

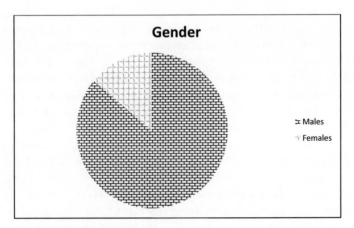

Source Research Data

6.4.2 Alliance engagement

With regards to strategic alliance fears it was expected that male and female responses would differ as women are more likely to be more cautious and build relationships over a period of time than men. Comparing the statistics for men and women it was seen that they shared similar concerns about forming alliances and the effect if might have on the business for example men and women showed similar concerns about the loss of control of their business men (n=246, 64.40%) women (n=37, 59.68%) similar scores were replicated across all the options under "concerns"

Table 6.4 Strategic alliance engagement concerns

Concern	Male	Female
Motivation of partner firm	312 (81.68%)	41 (66.13%)
Lack of ownership of innovation	222 (58.11%)	31 (50%)
Loss of control of business	246 (64.40%)	37 (59.68%)
Previous bad experience of partnership	177 (46.34%)	34 (54.84%)
Differences in values or goals	253 (66.23%)	39 (62.9%)

Source Research Data

6.4.3 Respondents age

Age is a frequently used variable in management research as people will become more strategic as they age and develop capabilities not always found in younger managers and older managers are more likely to be stable in their roles and therefore be more risk adverse.

Questions 1.2 asked participants to indicate their age band and to place themselves in a category rather than to write their age there were six categories to choose from. The age ranged from under 20 to over 60 and returned (Mean = 4.4 SD = 1.18). The respondents self reported themselves as belonging to the following groups <20 (n = 5, 1.1%), (21, 4.7%) reported themselves as between 21-30 years old, (n= 70, 15.8%) reported themselves as between 31-40, (n= 140, 31.5%) placed themselves in the age group 41-50 and (n = 114, 25.7%) indicated they were between 51 and 60 years of age, the rest placed them selves in the age band over 61+ (n = 94, 21.2%). Table 6.3 and figure 6.2 presents the data collected regarding age from the respondents. Age has been cross-tabbed with gender so that it can be easily seen the relationship between the age of the respondents and their gender. Most Female respondents reported themselves being between 31 and 50 placing themselves in the middle category. The men reported themselves as being mainly older. Means and standard deviations were also obtained for the demographic variables and the output is displayed in table 6.3. The data indicates that from the 444 respondents there is a mean of 1.14 and a standard deviation of .35. Figure 6.3 illustrates the industry type and age of the respondents to identify whether or not there is any significant difference in age of managers in certain types of industries.

Figure 6.2 Cross tabulation of age and gender

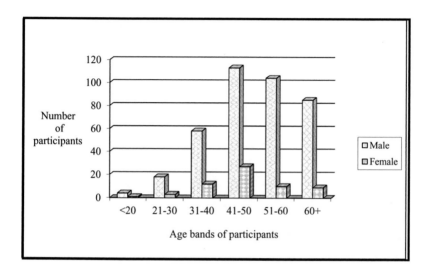

Source Research Data

Figure 6.3 Cross tabulation of manager's age and industry type

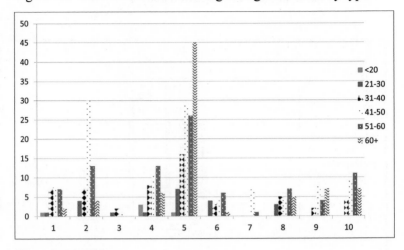

Source Research Data

Key

1   Nano Tech

2   Software tech

3   Gaming tech

4   Electronics

5   Tech dev

6   chem

7   Petro chem.

8   Pharmaceutical

9   Biological

10 Bio medical

6.4.4 Education

In the management literature, educational achievement has been considered an indicator of a persons general skills and knowledge. It is argued that owners of high tech firms have a higher level of education than may be found in managers of other types of firms. Question 1.3 asked respondents to indicate the highest education qualification they had obtained, The responses have been aggregated in table 6.3 and are presented in graphical form in figure 6.4 cross tabulated with gender, and in table 6.5 as percentages so that further comparison can be made. The education levels were broken up into groups that included secondary, further and higher education stages and included qualifications from GCSE O Levels or equivalent to postgraduate study. (Mean = 4.68 SD1.45) Fifteen (3.4%) reported that they had GCSE O Levels while (n = 26, 5.9%) had A Levels. Diplomas and others which included vocational training were (n = 30, 6.8%) and (n = 39, 39%) respectively. Those with degrees included undergraduate degrees (n = 127. 28.6%) masters (n = 102, 23%) and PhD (n=103, 23.6%).

28.6% of the total managers were found to have a minimum of an undergraduate degree men (n=111, 29.05%) women (n=16, 25.80%) with men who had a degree becoming managers at a younger age. For all the qualification options the percentages of men and women were similar indicating that in the high tech sector educational attainment is considered necessary. A significant number of managers with postgraduate degrees were found to be the owner and manager of the firm. Those managers with PhDs were found to be more likely to seek alliances for technological development. Age and attainment of these higher qualifications were found to impact on their decision to form alliances.

165

Figure 6.4 Cross tabulation of education and gender

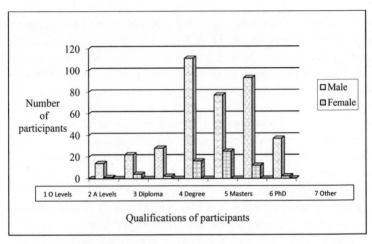

Source Research Data

Table 6.5   Educational achievement

Education \ Gender	O Levels	A Levels	Diploma	First Degree	Masters	PhD	Other
Males	14 (3.66%)	22 (5.76%)	28 (7.33%)	111 (29.05%)	77 (20.16%)	93 (24.35%)	37 (9.69)
Females	1 (1.61%)	4 (6.45%)	2 (3.22%)	16 (25.80%	25 (40.32%)	12 (19.35%)	2 (3.22%)

Source Research Data

6.4.5 Managerial experience

Question 1.5 asked participants to indicate how many years managerial experience they had the responses have been aggregated in table 6.3 and presented in figure 6.5. Some of the respondents indicated that their managerial experience started with their ownership of the business, for others they had accumulated a number of years experience and according to BERR (2008) entrepreneurs have usually held a directorship elsewhere prior to starting their own business. The majority of respondents indicated between 11 and 20 years experience which is consistent with the older age of respondents. The number of years of managerial experience was grouped into five categories giving (Mean 3.4, SD 1.52) 1-5 years, (n = 73, 16.4%), 6-10 years (n = 60, 13.5%, 11-15 years (n = 70, 15.8%), 16-20 years (n = 69, 15.5%), 20+ years (n = 167, 37.6%).

Figure 6.5 Cross tabulation of managerial experience and gender

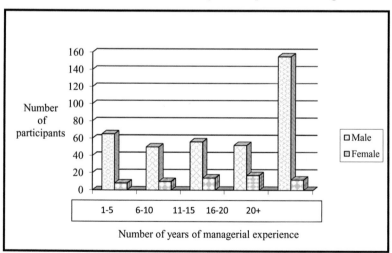

Source Research Data

167

6.4.6 Management

Prior studies (Byast and Karami, 2009) found that women were equally likely to be strategic planners cross tabulation of use of managerial tools and gender indicated that they were strategic planners as illustrated in figure 6.6. Furthermore the number of total responses was males 87% and Females 12.5%. The majority of males (n = 288, 93.75%) reported that alliances should form part of the firms overall strategy, (n = 40, 97.56%). The results for the importance of the use of strategic planning were aggregated in to very important and not important and are presented in the cross tabulation figure 6.7. The majority of males thought it was important to practice strategic planning (n = 302, 90.42%), the female scores were also high (n = 85.19%) indicating that they thought it was important to have strategic planning in place. The results of this is as expected i.e. managers in the high tech sector regardless of gender are likely to be formal planners and the importance of aligning alliance strategy with the business strategy (Berry and Taggart 1998).

Figure 6.6 Cross tabulation of need for alliance strategy to be integrated with the business strategy and gender

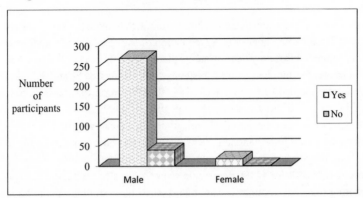

Source Research Data

Figure 6.7 Use of strategic planning and gender

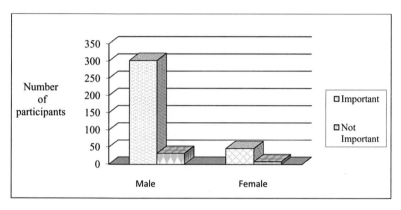

Source Research Data

6.5 Firm demographics

Questions two to question 15 from section two and questions one two and three from section three on the questionnaire were used to gain demographic information about the respondent firms. This data has been aggregated to produce a profile of the firms and a profile of their behaviour and these are presented in table 6.6 and table 6.7. Profiling the respondent firms in this manner enables the researcher to establish a model of firms operating in the high tech sector in the 21st Century. The collected data enables the researcher to draw conclusions about SMEs in the high tech sector and their strategic alliance success.

Table 6.6 provides a profile of the surveyed firms. These SMEs are characterised by the findings that the majority are run by the owner-manager in a personal way with direct control over all aspects of the business. These firms are operating in the high tech sector as indicated by SIC codes. As discussed in section 6.4 these firms are run by managers who significantly influence the firm through their attitudes and experience. Over a quarter of the firms are at their start up stage with a total of (n= 266, 77.32%) firms being under 10 years of age. The number of well established firms is (n= 89, 25.87%) with these reporting significant experience of successful strategic alliances. Prior research has focused on larger firms and excluded those with less than 10 employees.

From this study it is seen that over 60% of studied firms had less than five employees with a further 35.5% having up to 10 employees. Only 4.8% of the firms reported having over 100 employees this confirms that high tech SMEs tend to be smaller and more prolific than firms in other industries. Table 6.6 presents the data regarding alliance behaviour of the firms. Of the 402 who responded to the question about their involvement in strategic alliances, the majority (n=228 56.7%) have engaged in at least one alliance. Further analysis shows that these experienced firms are also those that attracted investment and reinvested in their firms. Of these firms a significant number also had at least one patent pending.

These descriptive statistics imply that there is a concentration of SMEs operating as technology development firms who are able to attract investment and engage in strategic alliances to remain competitive. These firms also have a range of products at different stages of development which confirms their propensity to innovation. The participants indicated a range of areas in which they were involved with planning activities. They placed emphasis on different factors which contributed to their use of planning. The participants indicated that as well as carrying out environmental scanning they also undertook trend analysis, competitor analysis and PESTLE analysis.

Table 6.6 Profile of respondent firms

Variable	Category	Frequency	Percentage	Mean	S.D.
Firm Age (n=420)	<5	117	27.9%	2.3	1.09
	+5-10	149	35.5%		
	11-20	65	15.5%		
	20+	89	21.2%		
Employees (n=420)	<5	260	61.9%	1.98	1.52
	6-10	51	12.1%		
	11-20	35	8.3%		
	21-50	26	6.2%		
	51-100	28	6.7%		
	101 or more	20	4.8%		
Industry (n=352)	Nano Tech	23	6.5%	5.08	2.57
	Software tech	58	16.5%		
	Gaming tech	4	1.1%		
	Electronics	42	11.9%		
	Tech dev	124	35.2%		
	chem	17	4.8%		
	Petro chem.	8	2.3%		
	Pharmaceutical	24	6.8%		
	Biological	21	6.%		
	Bio medical	31	8.8%		

Table 6.7 Profile of firm productivity and behaviour

Variable	Category	Frequency	Percentage	Mean	S.D.
Strategic Alliance (n=402)	No	174	43/3%		
	Yes	228	56.7%	1.43	.50
Investment Attracted (n=254)	5-50,000	149	68.7%		
	51,000 – 100,000	39	15.4%	1.42	.50
	100,000 or more	66	26.%		
Investment Made (n=315)	5-50,000	198	62.9%		
	51,000 – 100,000	54	17.1%	1.29	.46
	100,000 or more	63	20%		
Patents Received (n=133)	1	65	48.9%		
	2	31	23.3%	2.35	1.82
	3	7	5.3%		
	4	8	6.%		
	6 or more	22	16.5%		
Sales (n=147)	25,000	18	12.2%		
	40,000	12	8.2%	3.31	1.06
	80,000	24	16.3%		
	100,000	93	63.3%		

Source Research Data

*For the categories with missing data the valid percentage has been taken

6.5.1 Age of firm

The age of the company is an important demographic as young companies may not be able to attract investment and therefore not survive. On the other hand young successful companies may be easy targets for larger competitors who seek to take advantage of innovative capacity and who offer experience in exchange. Question 2.6 asked the manager to indicate how long the business had been in operation. The age of the company combined with the age of the manager may be a factor when considering alliances as a young firm with an experienced manager may be able to negotiate, implement and manage an alliance for the benefit of the firm whereas a younger inexperienced manager may fall prey to a larger firm seeking to obtain innovative capacity through alliance with a young innovative firm but who may not deliver its side of the agreement. The age of they surveyed firms are aggregated in table 6.6. It is observed that most of the sample firms are either very young and in their set up stage and are currently very innovative or are older well established companies who have accumulated a substantial amount of experience. Table 6.6 indicates that the age distribution is positively skewed with most of the SMEs being in their infancy.

6.5.2 Maturity of firm and business strategy

It was considered that the age of the firm would impact on the type of strategy that would be employed by the respondent firms. The younger firms i.e. <5 indicated that their strategy was to target a broader market (n = 50, 43%) while the older firms used product differentiation (n = 39, 45.89%) and broader markets (n = 35, 30%). The aggregated data is presented in table 6.9.

Table 6.9 Maturity of firms and business strategy

Strategy / Age of the firm	Local market	Broader market	Price	Product differentiation
<5	30	50	0	36
5-10	31	46	1	68
11-20	6	29	3	20
20+	10	30	6	39

Source Research Data

6.5.3 Firm size (indicated by employee numbers)

The number of employees is frequently used as a determinant of firm size and an increase or retention of employees may be an indication of the success of the company or may indicate its growth. As stated in the methodology independent owners were sought as unit of analysis and the findings here contradict those of Cooper (1973) where it was expected that high tech entrepreneurial firms would have multiple owners, perhaps reflected the changes in the industry in the last forty years. Question 2.7 asked participants to indicate how many employees they had so that the firms could be classified as micro, small or medium enterprises. The aggregated data is illustrated in figure 6.8 the majority of the firms would be categorised as micro businesses because of the number of employees reported as were below 10 indicating as expected that SMEs are abundantly found in the high tech sector (n=302. 74%) Small firms (n=60, 14%) Medium (n=48, 12%) (n=260 58.6%).

Figure 6.8 Firm classification as indicated by employee numbers

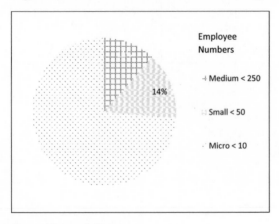

Source Research Data

6.5.4 Firm classification and firm age

Table 6.10 indicates the age of firm with employee numbers. The majority of young firms are classified as micro firms (n=108) with none of the new start ups being classified as medium and just (n=8) being classified as small. The majority of older firms were classified as medium based on the number of employees however these are not necessarily scientific or technical proficient staff as it would be expected that older firms would have more support staff for example human resources or marketing departments.

Table 6.10 Cross tabulation of firm classification and firm age

Firm age / Firm Classification	<5	+5-10	11-20	20+
Micro	108	108	55	31
Small	8	22	7	23
Medium	0	12	66	104

Source Research Data

6.5.6 Strategic management

The existing theories on strategic management were reviewed in chapters two and three and the perceptions of the importance of a manager understanding their environments were discussed. There are a number of models that can be used to assess a firms capabilities and these include SWOT analysis, PESTEL analysis, Porters Five Forces analysis to name but a few. It is important that a firm especially those in the competitive environment of high technology should be aware of threats and opportunities and how these will affect the business. Table 6.13 illustrates the frequency that the respondent firms carry out analysis to assist with strategic management and decision making. As indicated those that exercised environmental analysis experienced successful alliances (n-213 94.6%), However more firms considered competitor analysis as being beneficial to successful alliances. It can be concluded that firms who understand and work with their competitors will reap the benefits of sharing resource complementary activities.

6.5.7 Managerial decision making

Prior to making managerial decisions managers have access to a number of techniques to assist their decision making question 2.15 asked how important the different techniques were for their firm. Table 6.13 shows the aggregated responses from those that thought they were important to very important. 85.5% of the firms thought strategic business planning as important to their firms performance. 58.4% used PESTEL analysis to assist with managerial decision making. 79.7% stated that competitor analysis was very important.

The literature is divided about SMEs and their strategic planning reporting that management are significantly involved in strategic planning and this study revealed that of those who said they were the owner manager that 9.6%

of department managers are involved in planning while a further 8.3% said that consultants were used. Previous chapters i.e. one, three and four have discussed the characteristics of managers which will influence their strategic planning approach. There is a growing body of literature regarding the influence and importance of top management teams rather than an individual.

6.5.8 SME managers: crisis managers or strategists?

Analysis of the responses of the respondents indicated that managers of SMEs in the high tech sector tend to be more strategists than crisis managers when asked to consider whether or not strategic alliances should be built into their overall strategic plan the majority answered that they thought it should. Table 6.13 illustrates the importance attached to the use of business tools by the studied firms.

Table 6.13 Employment of management tools

Technique Applied	Frequency		Successful alliances	Mean	S.D.
Environmental Analysis	225 (58.4%)		213 (94.6%)	2.61	1.31
Competitor Analysis	311 (79.7%)		215 (69.10%)	2.14	1.23
Strategic planning	332 (85.5%)		218 (65.55%)	1.86	1.04
Business Trend Analysis	271(70.2%)		216 (79.70%)	2.31	1.21
Industry Analysis	290 (74.8%)		220 (75.86%)	2.18	1.08
Do you create a profile of your prospective partners?	Yes	No		1.58	.50
	137 (42%)	189 (58%			
Should strategic alliance be part of the overall strategy	Yes	No		1.06	.23
	119 (95.2%	6 (4.8%)			

Source Research Data

Table 6.19 provides a profile of the surveyed firms strategic alliance behaviour. Over a quarter of the firms are at their start up stage with a total of 266 firms being under 10 years of age. The number of well-established firms is 89 with these reporting significant experience of successful strategic alliances.

Table 6.19 Profile of alliance behaviour

Variable	Category	Frequency	Percentage	Mean	S.D.
Create a profile of the prospective partner	Yes	137	42%		
	No	189	58%	1.58	.49
Alliance experience	Yes	228	56.7%	1.43	.50
	No	174	43.3%		
Who instigates the alliance (Experienced Firms)	Manager	180	82.95%		
	Dept Manager	23	10.6%	1.34	.63
	Consultant	14	6.45%		
Motives for cooperation by respondent firm	Market Access	155	45%		
		77	22%	2.26	1.42
	Customer Access	38	10%		
	Finance for	38	10%		
	R&D	43	13%		
	Technology Transfer				
	Knowledge Transfer				
Perception of benefit from strategic alliances	Marketing	319	63.3%	1.95	1.08
	Financial	258	51.1%	2.34	1.22
		252	50.0%	2.33	1.22

183

	Technology Transfer	181	35.9%	2.83	1.25

Source Research Data

Profile continued

Variable	Category	Frequency	Percentage	Mean	S.D.
	Based in cluster	336	66.6%	1.47	.71
Success factors of alliances	Technological compatibility	283	46.2	2.20	1.08
	Geographical proximity	164	31.9%	3.02	1.41
	Mutual trust	348	69.1	1.41	.76
	Resource complementary	284	56.4%	1.95	1.01
	Management styles compatible	305	60.5%	2.00	.98
	Flexibility and compatibility	331	65.6%	1.72	.84
Failure Factors of Alliances	Seeking quick financial gain	273	44.2%	2.09	1.17
	Problems with decision making due to hierarchy	338	67.0%	1.74	.80

	Partners not fulfilling role	331	65.6%	1.72	.81
	High dependency on partner	279	55.3%	2.06	.93

Source Research Data

6.6.2 Success factors for strategic alliance formation

Managerial perceptions were measured regarding the critical success factors for strategic alliances. The managers reported that mutual trust is considered the most significant factor with (n=348 69.1%) while geographical proximity was considered the least factor contributing towards success of an alliance with only (n=164 31.9%), this result finds confirmation from prior research for example Chen and Karami (2010). However the least observed variance was for the success factors related to being in a cluster of similar firms suggesting there was agreement that this is considered an important factor for the respondent firms. It would appear that having firms that are similar to their own means that relationships can be built up over time while for the facilitation of an alliance then companies do not need to be in close proximity to each other. This distance is lessened by the use of supporting infrastructures such as electronic communication, high speed deliveries and the use of mobile labour.

6.6.3 Engagement in alliances

The majority of the respondent firms indicated that they were experienced in terms of having engaged in alliances (n=228 56.7%). Of these it was thought that a profile of the characteristics required in a prospective partner was beneficial (n=137 42%) The majority of the managers of experienced firms stated that they instigate the alliance themselves with a minority saying they had used a consultant. Market access was the prominent determinant for engaging in alliances for all firms while the younger firms also emphasised the importance of alliances for financing their research and development, requiring both technology and knowledge transfer from the relationships.

6.6.8 Success factors of alliances

As discussed in previous sections motivations for avoiding or engaging in alliances are diverse as are the perceptions about the benefits of an alliance, question 3.10 explores the area of what might contribute to an alliances success. The results for this question are displayed in table 6.22. It is important that the manager is committed to the alliance and the results indicate through self reporting by the managers that they are motivated to forming alliances in areas that they lack competency and they view managerial compatibility between the partnering firms as important. Analysing the responses from the respondents it is apparent that managers in high tech firms perceive trust to be an important factor in strategic alliance success. The responses are similar for both experienced and inexperienced firms, there is the assumption that people behave in an appropriate way and is linked to common human behaviour.

6.6.9 Failure factors of alliances

The factors which contribute to failure may not necessarily be those opposite that contribute to alliance success question 3.11 asks what firms rate as contributing to the failure those responses that were important or above have been aggregated in table 6.23.

Analysing the responses from the respondents it is apparent that managers in high tech firms perceive the lack of trust as causing failure of alliances. They self reported that they did not view geographical proximity as important to an alliance, however it was also not a detriment to the alliance.

188

6.6.10 Factors of importance when considering an alliance

As already discussed perceptions of managers about the needs and benefits of alliances are diverse and therefore so may be the factors that influence their decision making about alliance formation question 3.13 asks managers how important certain factors were when considering alliances, those that were rated important or above are aggregated into table 6.23. As can be seen a low response was received for reducing competitive pressure this may suggest that firms do not form alliances with their competitors. The majority of respondents self reported that the need for access to customers, speed of entry to market all influence their decision making when considering strategic alliances. Complex tasks also result in firms with little knowledge about certain processes will lead them to seek alliances as will the willingness to share risks.

6.7 Chapter summary

In this chapter the survey data collected by means of the postal questionnaire has been analysed. This chapter has provided descriptive statistics for the aggregated data such as cross tabulation, means and standard deviation displaying the output in tables and graphs. Displaying the data in this way has made comparison of the results easy to identify. Using the collected data it has been possible to draw up a profile of the managers and firms operating in the high tech sector in the United Kingdom. The demographics and background characteristics of the respondents, their firms and alliance behaviour have been included in this chapter and chapter seven will statistically analyse the data in order to answer the research questions and test the hypothesis. Chapter eight will provide some discussion on the findings and synbooke them with incumbent literature.

Chapter Seven: Statistical Data Analysis

7.1   Introduction

The methodology for data collection was discussed fully in chapter five. Chapter six presented descriptive analysis of the data and explored some possible links between the variables. This chapter addresses the research questions and carries out the statistical data analysis and tests the hypothesis associated with each research objective.   Non parametric statistical techniques have been utilised in the absence of normality of the data.   The chapter concludes with a summary of the statistical analysis and is followed by chapter eight where the findings are discussed.

7.1.1 Reliability statistics

T tests that were carried out to indicate that there are no significant differences of the effect males and females have on decision making and alliance formation. It is assumed for this study that the sample method has returned owners as individuals rather than partnerships although it is found by others that successful small firms are founded by small partnerships or teams of between two and five members (Cooper, 1973).

7.1.2 T tests and independence of variables

It was necessary to investigate whether two independent variables may have an effect on each other. To explore the independence of the genders i.e. are men more likely to form alliances than women t-tests were carried out to test independence i.e. to establish whether there is a relationship between gender and alliance formation, the information is displayed in table 7.1. After checking the information about the groups to ensure that there were not any missing values assumptions about the equality of the variances was checked. This is determined by the sig. value as indicated in the shaded area in table 7.1 as .421 as this is larger than .05 it is assumed that the variance of the scores for males and females is the same and no violations have occurred. The t-test for equality of means returned a figure of .003 which indicates a significant difference in the means scores on the dependant variable by each of the groups i.e. males and females. As there were many more males than females in the study looking at the percentages show that the differences are not that wide. Given the low ratio between males and female respondents this is not a major significance. T tests that were carried out to indicate that there are no significant differences of the effect males and females have on decision making and alliance formation.

Table 7.1 Testing for variances independent samples test

		Levene's test for equality of variances		t-test for equality of means		
		F	Sig	t	df	Sig (2 tailed)
Have you engaged in any alliances ?		Lower	Upper	Lower	Upper	Lower
		.650	.421	-3.020	400	.003
	Equal variance			-3.029	68.90	.003

	not assumed					

Source Research Data

7.1.3 Hypothesis testing and correlation analysis

Correlation analysis is used to describe the strength and direction of a relationship between two variables. For the purpose of this study Spearman rank order correlation is carried out to explore the strength of the relationship between continuous variables to test the hypothesis.

7.2 Research questions

The research question was formulated in chapter one to help address the gap in the literature on strategic alliance behaviour in the smaller SME in the high tech sector in the UK. As discussed reasons for failure have previously been the focus for researchers with little attention paid to characteristics and motivations that might affect engagement in alliance, the monitoring and evaluation of the alliance, which might result in alliance success. There are two research questions and four research objectives. To enable the carrying out of the research objectives six hypotheses have been compiled. Two of the hypothesis is related to research question one and four to research question two.

7.2.1 Research question one

This section addresses the proposition associated with research question one and the related research objectives and hypothesis. These are presented in table 7.2.

Research Proposition 1 Identify key demographics of owner managers including gender, age, education and managerial experience to establish the affect that these demographics and background characteristics have on strategic alliance. To do this a profile of both managers of small high tech firms and the firms themselves were created in chapter six to give a definition of a owner manager of a small high tech firm operating in the turbulent environment of the high tech industry today.

Table 7.2 Research question one and related objectives and hypothesis

Research Question	Research Objectives	Hypothesis
How do management and firm demographics affect strategic alliance success in the high tech sector?	**Research Objective 1** To investigate the relationship between demographics and background characteristics of managers and strategic alliance success.	**Hypothesis 1** H_1 There is significant correlation between demographics and background characteristics of managers and strategic alliance success.
	Research Objective 2 To investigate the relationship between demographics and background characteristics of firms and strategic alliances.	**Hypothesis 2** H_2 There is significant correlation between firm's demographics and background characteristics and successful strategic alliances.

7.2.1.1   Research objective one - hypothesis one

The relationship between the individual manager's demographics and background characteristics and their experience of alliance success was investigated using Spearman's Rho. Preliminary analyses were performed to ensure no violation of the assumptions of normality, linearity and homoscedasticity. The independent variables chosen were gender age, educational attainment, managerial experience and the independent variables were engagement in successful strategic alliances and the creation of a profile of the prospective partner prior to engagement. The output is presented in figure 7.1.

Figure 7.1 illustrates that there is a significant correlation between a manager's gender and successful alliances. The age of the managers and therefore their experience will influence their willingness to engage in alliances is strongly correlated. From the summary, this study can report that an individuals' demographics alone do not significantly affect their alliance success but that background characteristics such as experience influence their alliance success. Those who entered alliances also demonstrate a small correlation with creating a profile of potential partners. It was felt that comparing the correlation coefficients for males and females and their decision to engage in alliances would give a useful insight to what extent gender influences management decision making. The output for creating a profile suggests that women might embark on and manage their alliances differently.

The relationship between the manager's demographics and background characteristics and their strategic alliance success was investigated using Spearman's rank order correlation. The independent variables chosen were manager's gender, age, education and managerial experience. The dependant variables were strategic alliance success. The output is displayed in figure 7.1.

Figure 7.1 Spearman's Rank Order correlation matrix for demographics and alliance

	1	2	3	4	5	6
1 Gender	1					
2 Age	-.105*	1				
3 Education	-.004	.152**	1			
4 Experience	-.071	.627**	.046	1		
5 Alliance Success	.149**	-.180**	-.071	-.145**	1	
6 Profile	-.081	.030	.127*	-.019	.171**	1

** Correlation is significant at the 0.01 level (2-tailed).

* Correlation is significant at the 0.05 level (2-tailed).

The hypothesis that there is significant correlation between managers demographics and background characteristics and alliance success is supported by a positive relationship between gender ($\gamma=149**$ p>0.01) and a negative relationship age ($\gamma=-.180**$p>0.01) and experience, ($\gamma=-.145*$ p>0.01) and alliance success.

It is considered that a manager's age is correlated with their ability to innovate, spearman rank order correlation was carried out to test the relationship between a manager's age and their ability to be innovative. There is correlation between a managers age and stages of development ($\gamma=.748**$ p>0.01). Younger managers did not have any correlation with registrations or getting the products to market.

Figure 7.2 Correlation between manager's age and ability to innovate

	1	2	3	4	5	6	7	8
1 Age	1	.118	.120	.439**	.514**	.026	.129	-.161
2 R&D	.118	1	.748**	.744**	.647**	.479*	.523*	.121
3 Development	.120	.748**	1	.821**	.718**	.619*	.715*	.321*
4 Trials	.439**	.744**	.821**	1	.845**	.416	.540*	-.223
5 Clinical	.514**	.647**	.718**	.845**	1	.212	.344	.121
6 Registration	.026	.479(**)	.619(**)	.416	.212	1	.900(**)	.394(*)
7 Patent	.129	.523(**)	.715(**)	.540(**)	.344	.900(**)	1.000	.216
8 Marketing	-.161	.121	.321(**)	-.223	.121	.394(*)	.216	1.000

** Correlation is significant at the 0.01 level (2-tailed).

* Correlation is significant at the 0.05 level (2-tailed).

7.2.1.2   Research objective two - hypothesis two

The relationship between the individual firm's demographics and background characteristics and their experience of alliance success was investigated using Spearman's Rank order correlation. The independent variables chosen were the firm's age, size, Location, firm's capabilities and managerial experience and the dependent variables were engagement in successful strategic alliances. The output is presented in figure 7.3.

Hypothesis two is supported as there is significant correlation between a firms size and its age ($\gamma=.440^{**}$ p>001) and there is a correlation between success and age ($\gamma=.216^{**}$ p>001) indicating that the older the firm is then it is morel likely to engage in successful strategic alliances. There is also significant correlation between firm size and alliance success ($\gamma=.209^{**}$ p>001) suggesting that the larger a firm (in terms of employee numbers) is the easier it will be for the manager to handle a strategic alliance.

Figure 7.3 Correlation matrix for firm age, size and success in alliances

	1age	2size	3success
1Age	1		
2Size	.440**	1	
3Success	.216**	.209**	1

** Correlation is significant at the 0.01 level (2-tailed).

* Correlation is significant at the 0.05 level (2-tailed).

The hypothesis that there is significant correlation between firm's demographics and background characteristics and successful strategic alliances is strongly supported by the firm's size and its age.

198

To further examine correlations between a firm's demographics and activities correlation was carried out between the firm's size and activities, the output is presented in figure 7.4. The results identify some significant correlations between firm size, and its activities Development Research (γ=179* p>.0.05), R&D (γ=228**p>0.01), Product Development (γ=229**p>0.01), clinical trials (γ=380**p>0.01), Patent Application (γ=418**p>0.1), marketing (γ=316**p>0.01). Therefore, hypothesis two is supported on all counts except marketing activities, this shows that marketing is a weak area for the firms as self-reported by the managers.

Figure 7.4 Correlation between a firm's age, size and its activities

		1	2	3	4	5	6	7	8	9	10	11
1	Age	1										
2	Size	.440**	1									
3	Development Research	.135	.179*	1								
4	R & D	.167*	.228**	.710**	1							
5	Development	.136	.229**	.721**	.748**	1						
6	Clinical or other trials	.362*	.380**	.709**	.647**	.718**	1					
7	Other Trials	.086	.070	.837**	.744**	.821**	.845**	1				
8	Patent Application	.139	.418**	.536**	.523**	.715**	.344	.540**	1			
9	Registration	.147	.274	.269	.479**	.619**	.212	.416	.900**	1		
10	Marketing	.047	.171*	.109	.121	.321*	.121	.223	.216	.394*	1	
11	Successful Strategic Alliance	.247*	.316**	.285*	.321*	.426*	.526*	.887*	.448**	.829**	073	1

200

** Correlation is significant at the 0.01 level (2-tailed).

*Correlation is significant at the 0.05 level (2-tailed).

Through empirical findings it is clear that firms who engage in strategic planning, build up a profile of prospective partner are able to engage in successful strategic alliances, it is therefore considered in this research whether or not identifying at the start of the business alliance needs and aligning them with the business strategy would contribute to the alliance success. A positive outcome would confirm that those SME owners who align their strategic planning, employ at least one business tool to identify the competition or to investigate the market are strategic planners from the outset and less likely to be managers of crisis. Results of the correlation matrix for including alliance as strategy with alliance success revealed a weak positive association (γ=.173 p>0.01) between strategic planning and aligning their strategic alliances following an analysis of the environment in which they operate confirms that SME managers in the high tech sector in the UK are strategic planners and enjoy successful alliances through careful planning and monitoring of the alliance.

Figure 7.9 Correlation matrix to establish the relationship between a manager's motivation towards the strategic alliance and firm performance

		1	2	3	4	5	6	7
1..Management Support	Correlation	1						
	Sig.	.						
2 Management Style	Correlation	.043	1					
	Sig.	.470						
3 Dependency on partner	Correlation	.076	.390**	1				
	Sig.	.203	.000					
4 Degree of technology	Correlation	-.165**	.119*	.011	1			
	Sig.	.005	.024	.838				
5 Meeting Objectives	Correlation	.182**	.512**	.238**	.071	1		
	Sig.	.002	.000	.000	.177			
6 Customer Satisfaction	Correlation	.012	.042	.057	-.035	-.014	1	
	Sig.	.864	.489	.340	.556	.816		
7 Employee Satisfaction	Correlation	.014	.124	-.107	-.115	-.044	.370**	1
	Sig.	.843	.045	.085	.060	.482	.000	

** Correlation is significant at the 0.01 level (2-tailed).

* Correlation is significant at the 0.05 level (2-tailed).

Fig 7.10 Correlation matrix for degree of dependency on partners, loss of control and willingness to invest internally

	1	2	3	4
1 Experienced Firm	1			
2 Internal Investment	.044	1		
3 Loss of control	-.027	-.044	1	
4 High dependency on partner	-.192**	-.041	.111*	1

** Correlation is significant at the 0.01 level (2-tailed).

* Correlation is significant at the 0.05 level (2-tailed).

A manager who is motivated to form alliances would also display concerns and expectations about the outcome of the alliance and the behaviour of the prospective partner. These motivations and critical success factors would have an impact on firm performance as it would be thought the managers motives would have an impact on the alliance, the employees and the business generally, table 7.4 illustrates the motives for alliance formation as perceived by the managers. The areas that the managers are motivated to form an alliance differ across the industries and also reflect the current need of the firm.

Table 7.4 The motives for alliance formation

Market Access	Market Access	Customer Access	Finance for R&D	Technology Transfer	Knowledge Transfer
Research	X	X	X	X	X

R&D	✓(.752**)	X	✓(.775**)	✓(.966**)	✓(.673)
Developme nt	✓(.719**)	✓(.685**)	✓(.936**)	✓(915**)	X
Clinical Trials	X	✓(1.000**)	X	✓(.926**)	X
Other Trials	✓(.810**)	✓(1.000**)	X	✓(1.000**)	✓(.832**)
Patent	✓(.704**)	✓(1.000**)	✓(.926**)	✓(.905**)	✓(-.693*)
Registration	X	✓(1.000**)	X	X	X
Marketing	X	✓(.895**)	X	X	X

Source Research Data

Respondents were asked to indicate their motivations for seeking alliances. The percentage of firms who gave a motive are displayed in table 7.5. More experienced firms are more likely to see an alliance as a positive move to gain access to new markets and customers. The surprising result is that many experienced firms also look for finance and technology assistance through an alliance. The results are as expected when it comes to inexperienced firms seeking alliances for knowledge transfer, this result indicates that firms can learn from experienced partners and benchmarking best practice can help firms to be more successful.

Table 7.5 Firm's motivation for seeking alliances

	Firm Status	Number	%

Requirement from Alliance			
Market Access	Experienced Firm	108	50.94
	Inexperienced Firm	47	33.81
Customer Access	Experienced Firm	40	18.86
	Inexperienced Firm	37	26.61
Finance	Experienced Firm	25	11.79
	Inexperienced Firm	13	9.35
Technology Transfer	Experienced Firm	27	12.73
	Inexperienced Firm	11	7.91

Knowledge Transfer	Experienced Firm	12	5.66
	Inexperienced Firm	31	22.3

Source Research Data

Among the firms who are counted as experienced, i.e. they had engaged in alliances 51% chose market access as their primary motive for alliances while of the inexperienced firms 34% said that they would seek an alliance for market access. Customer access was considered important for both groups while 12.73% of experienced firms said they would seek an alliance for technology transfer and 11.79% said they would form an alliance for finance for research and development however 22.30% of inexperienced firms said they would form an alliance to gain knowledge from a partner.

7.2.2   Hypothesis outcome

Each of the hypothesis have been tested and all hypothesis have been accepted with some having stronger support than others by the association between the variables. Hypothesis one and two are strongly supported by managerial and firm demographics and therefore accepted.

H_1 There is significant correlation between demographics and background characteristics of managers and strategic alliance success.

Strongly supported by the managers age and education.

H_2 There is significant correlation between firms demographics and background characteristics and successful strategic alliances.

Strongly supported by the firm's size .and its age,

7.3   Chapter summary

This chapter has provided statistical analysis for the data collected through a postal survey targeting SMEs in the high tech sector in the UK. Using correlation analysis the hypothesis have been tested and the results are summarised together with an indication of support for the hypothesis. Results indicated that managerial and firm demographics have a significant impact on alliance success and firm performance, however it was also seen that environmental factors also are considered important considerations when making management decisions. Chapter eight will provide discussion on the findings and synthesisee them with incumbent literature.

Chapter Eight: Findings and discussions

8.1 Introduction

The methodology that was employed for this empirical research was discussed in chapter five and used in chapters six and seven to analyse the data collected through a postal survey of high tech firms in the UK. This chapter will review the research questions and discuss the findings presented via descriptive and statistical data analysis and illustration in chapters six and seven. This chapter will interpret the data and synthesise it with incumbent literature and prior research.

Variables for measuring management were identified in the conceptual framework and the questions around whether a managers demographics influence their decisions to form alliances and what motivates an individual to engage in or avoid alliances? The literature review highlighted that management demographics are considered important in decision making and influencing a firm's ability to grow. The deterministic approach to business growth (Dobbs and Hamilton, 2007) requires a set of stable variables to carry out the research. They suggest these variables relate to the manager, the firm's, and the industry in which it operates. This is the preferred model and the rational for the research objectives one and two and explores what causes growth rather than focusing on business learning and adaptation for growth.

Reviewing empirical research indicates that the usual variables for explaining small business growth are strategic management, demographics of the manager, firm's demographics and industry demographics.

According to Dodourova (2009), success and failure factors are closely related to management perceptions that are formed from a range of managerial demographics and background characteristics such as age and experience. According to (Kathuria et al, 2003; Carmen et al, 2006; Kauer et al, 2007; Goll et al, 2008) a managers demographics including tenure and education are likely to have a positive effect on firm performance and that managers can exploit these capabilities to gain competitive advantage through strategic alliance formation. The majority of these papers while providing some useful insights into management behaviour focused their research on teams rather than individuals.

Contemporary literature has begun to focus on the success factors of strategic alliances whether critical or not for example (Lunnan and Haugland, 2007; Jaouen and Gundolf, 2009; Chen and Karami, 2010). Prior empirical research into management and strategic alliance has focused on the success of the alliance through careful management (Mellat-Parast and Digman, 2007), Research and Development needs (Shefer and Frenkel, 2005), innovation (Nieto, 2004) partnering experience (Beverland and Bretherton, 2001; Smith, 2003) while management research has focused on larger firms emphasising the organisation, human resource and management capabilities together with the implementation of strategic management. (March and Gunasekaran, 1999; Grawe et al, 2009) while the more limited research into SMEs and alliances has focused on specific industries, use of ICT as a prescription to assist alliances (Mandal et al, 2003) more recently some attention has been paid towards specific pre alliance needs of SMEs and how they may form alliances with larger firms (Das and He 2006) this does not seek to explain the way that SMEs collaborate with each other and what their motivations for doing so are, finally a review of theories and their usefulness for SMEs (Hagerdoorn and Schakenraad, 1994; Berry, 1996; Berry and Taggart, 1998; Das and Teng, 2000; Rogers, 2001).

To bridge gaps highlighted by these researchers as discussed in chapters one and two this research focuses on SMEs and their managers perceptions and motivations for following strategic management practices and more specifically in the formation of strategic alliances to maximise their resources, share risks and learn from their partners. This chapter synthesise the empirical research findings in chapter six to the research aims and objectives of this study within the conceptual framework, existing literature the research proposition and the objective of the research.

The propositions are revisited together with their related research objective to present findings and interpretations of the aggregated results and whether they conform to literature or present contradictory findings. As reiterated throughout this study the dearth of literature directly relating to management decision making and strategic alliance formation the literature review and conceptual framework has had to rely on the general strategic management and alliance literature and research.

With reference to the specific objectives of this research, this chapter presents in more detail the findings presented in chapter six and seven together with interpretations for the results obtained that relate to the propositions. The chapter is divided into two main parts that address the two research questions and their related propositions. The research questions, the objectives and their propositions are restated below and are discussed during the remainder of the chapter. In summary this chapter discuses the findings of the data analysed in chapter six and seven together with interpretation for the findings relating to strategic management and strategic alliance formation in SMEs in the high tech sector.

8.2 Research Question

How do management and firm's demographics affect strategic alliance success in the high tech sector?

Strategic alliances help organisations to compete during environmental changes and turbulence giving them access to resources that will help them extend their businesses and enhancing their business capabilities while utilising those of their customers, suppliers and even competitors through alliances (Soosay et al, 2008; Calof and Wright, 2008).

Prior research into strategy and alliances (Barnes, 2001; Garengo and Bititci, 2007; Karami, 2007; O'Regan et al, 2008) have used manufacturing firms as a unit of analysis while high tech research have focused on the scope of R&D alliances (Oxley and Sampson, 2004) Knowledge Access and Transfer (Petruzzelli et al, 2007; Marshall, 2008) factors of failure (Mitsuhashi, 2002; Byast et al, 2010; Chao, 2011). Factors influencing partner selection (Rothaermel and Boeker, 2008; Sha and Swaminathan, 2008), management capabilities (Deeds et al, 1999; Schreiner et al, 2008; Lin et al, 2009; Srikan and MCGahan, 2010) and as a tribute to the need to understand organisational culture and its impact on alliances and changes that occur internally as a result (Leisen et al, 2002; Ghosh, 2004; Pansiri, 2005) all these are built from strong foundations of management theory from stalwarts such as Drucker, Porter and Mintzberg. This prior research has prompted research question one as it is not clear how much of the decision making is made from clear knowledge of the environment through environmental analysis or justified through prior experience and human frailties distinctive through the managers own demographics and background characteristics (Yordanova and Alexandrova-Boshnakova, 2011). It is acknowledged and supported through this research that for the majority that all firm's decisions are the economic and emotional concern of the manger from starting the business, location, driving forces, decision making and choices for strategic growth or to remain small and sustainable and each of these is influenced by the managers perceptions and analysis of the environment whether or not they are aware of it.

Proposition 1 Identify key demographics of owner managers including gender, age, education and managerial experience to establish the affect that these demographics and background characteristics have on firm's performance and strategic alliance success.

8.2.1 Research objective one

To investigate the relationship between demographics and background characteristics of managers and strategic alliance success.

Dodevurada (2009) reports significant findings that management characteristics directly influence management decision making.

Table 8.1 Hypothesis one

Hypothesis	Outcome
H_1 There is significant correlation between demographics and background characteristics of managers and strategic alliance success.	Hypothesis one is strongly supported by age and experience, gender also support the hypothesis However,, this is related to the different practices employed by the managers depending on their gender and their different expectations.

8.2.1.1   Discussion for research objective one – hypothesis one

The following section discusses the findings for hypothesis one. The outcomes are discussed in relation to existing literature and research and identifies confirmation of results or explains the differences.

8.2.1.1.1 Gender

Research into gender has focused on the failings of women to reach managerial positions, be pushed into self-employment for economic reasons and failed to perceive women for what they are an important element in the current labour market meaning that the literature into their decision making is scarce (Byast and Karami, 2009; Yordanova and Alexandrova-Boshnakova, 2011) and Catley and Hamilton (1998) who stressed the need for gender specific research. Research by Yordanova and Alexandrova-Boshnakova (2011) investigated the effects of gender on perceptions and willingness to take risks. Their findings concluded that "male and female entrepreneurs do not differ in their risk perception of business situations" despite this "female entrepreneurs exhibit lower risk propensity than male entrepreneurs" which supports this research highlighting the fact that women will act in similar ways to men but take more precautionary measures when setting up alliances for example creating a profile of their preferred partner, support that men and women hold different beliefs and will therefore act differently in similar situations comes from Granrose (2007).

In relation to the conceptual framework developed in chapter four the independent variables identified as most influential on firm performance were those associated with individuals and pertained to their demographic characteristics. It is confirmed that when the managers of SMEs in the high tech sector are experienced and have a certain level of education attainment then they are likely to be open to strategic alliance formation and will have the ability to maintain the relationship. Contrary to expectations, many do have the ability to broker the alliance and they perceive that as long as all partners are equally motivated to the alliance and have expectations of similar outcomes then all things being equal the alliance is likely to be successful. Managerial characteristics as an influence on decision making are widely researched and this study has confirmed that this is justified. Results are confirmatory to the incumbent literature that manager's individuality and the perceptions generated by this individuality will reflect on their management decision making. The majority of males thought it was important to practice strategic planning (n = 302, 90.42%), the female scores were also high (n = 85.19%) indicating that they thought it was important to have strategic planning in place. The results of this is as expected i.e. managers in the high tech sector regardless of gender are likely to be formal planners and the importance of aligning alliance strategy with the business strategy (Berry and Taggart, 1998). This reinforces the research by March and Gunasekaran (1999) who explored the strategic practices of managers in the high tech sector and stated that small firm's managers are more likely to be more strategic than previously considered (O'Regan and Ghobadian, 2002).

Motivation for women starting their own businesses have not featured greatly in literature and Walker and Webster (2007) provide evidence that women do not proactively seek to become self employed but do so because of economic factors or a lack of opportunities available to them that can be built around other domestic duties or as a means to inclusion the alternative to which is social exclusion (Stewart et al, 2003) and a social stigma and label as focused on by earlier work for (Marlow, 2006) However,, when identifying managerial qualities Carmichael 1995 suggest that men and women both have similar characteristics that make them both managers this study also identifies that despite the scarcity of females in this study men and women in the high tech sector think and act in a similar way support for this comes from Eagly and Johnson, (1990) who suggest that the similarities that exist between men and women tend to outweigh the differences. They suggest that more important characteristics such as the industry type etc may have more influence on their behaviour, support comes from Carmichael (1995) who suggests that there are characteristics that are inherent in either gender which would create good managers and agrees to some extent that within certain industries that managerial characteristics are more than the sum of gender, age and education.

It has been suggested in prior literature (Karami 2007) that the industry sector can influence the number of female managers and therefore the number of responses that this survey returned from female owner managers came as no surprise. Further more Semta (2010) found that only 21% of Semta's workforce in the UK is female compared to 48% for all sectors in the UK also in other research (Langowitz and Minniti, 2007; Dvir et al, 2010) found relatively low percentages of women in their studies.

From this survey of managers in the high tech sector the majority of the respondents were males with only 14% of the respondents were female. This result confirms that men are more likely to be found as owner managers in high tech industries as reported by Karami (2007) in his study based on the SET industries where the respondents were mostly male. Similarly, a report by BERR (2008) found women were under represented in their sample of UK high growth firms as did research by Yahaya and Abu-Bakar (2007); However,,, research on female decision makers returned a reputable sample Ndemo and Maina (2007). Hypothesis one was supported by gender having an influence on strategic alliance formation, what varied was the way in which the genders approached the relationship. Lasch, et al (2007) report that gender does not influence success but that there is a significant difference in the number of start-ups between the genders as is between their fears about long term sustainability rather than growth but also posit fears that these firms are more likely to fail than survive. This may explain to some extent why the women who were generally younger than the male respondents were more likely to create a profile of their intended partner as lack of experience would mean that they would need something prescriptive to base their judgement on.

Furthermore Semta (2010) found that the effect of the gender on growth performance was positive for males while female entrepreneurs were found to have lower growth ambitions, this study reveals that for the respondents this was not the case as both men and women self-reported the achievement of goals these results find support from (Byast and Karami, 2009; Vaidya et al, 2011; Weeks, 2009,) who found that most women surveyed were optimistic about their futures and focused on growth, However,, Vaidya (2011) found that the use of managerial tools differed between the genders.

Further support for this research comes from Cohoon et al (2010) whose longitudinal study of 549 high tech firms compared the backgrounds, experiences and motivation of men and women and found that they were similar in both demographics and background characteristics but displayed some different business behaviour in so far as women were motivated in different ways and had prior preparation before selecting a partner these differences in the gender may prompt different variables to be tested in future research.

For the women who self-reported as managers in a certain age group the percentages are more uniform and women in all age groups are equally well represented. Given the relatively small number of women respondents it is clear that women owner managers in the high tech sector are equally likely to be found as men during the early years of the business when other commitments may not detract from their ability to manage a business in a sector where women managers are less evident than men (Karami, 2007).

8.2.1.1.2 Manager's age, experience and strategic alliance behaviour

There is evidence from literature that management qualities that come from characteristics such as age, education and experience are to be found in successful firms and that managers with these qualities are more likely to be open to alliance formation (Dodevurada, 2009; Yordanova and Alexandrova-Boshnakova, 2011). The characteristics that most influence the decision-making are managerial experience and age of the manager. There is no statistical difference in the adoption of strategic management between the genders and it is considered that SME owners are likely to replicate successful practices of other firms benchmarked against all industrial sectors and not just in the high tech sector, particularly women are identified in the service sector as formal strategists (Byast and Karami, 2009).

Results in chapter six reveal two distinct groups of SME owner in the high tech sector and this is supported by Giacon (2008) who found four types, which included those who had left academia to start up a high tech business and family run firms.

- "the emergent young entrepreneur; young people with smart ideas, sometimes highly educated, (PhD or master degree) who are able to build, in a few years, rapid growing businesses. They are particular diffused in the ICT world" Giacon (2008) the managers in this study confirms this as many are found in the new technology development industries which suggests that younger managers may typically be innovative, there is also a large number of older managers which may reflect Giacon's ex academic in the technology development.

- "former manager or scientist who create a spin-off. This typology is quite popular within the biotech and pharmaceutical world" Giacon (2008) and this supports findings in this study as more older experienced managers are prevalent in the pharmaceutical, biological and bio medical industries"

Semta (2010 p5)also found correlation with ages in these sectors Only 9% of Semta's workforce in the UK is aged 16-24 compared to 14% for all sectors in the UK. 14% of Semta's workforce in the UK is aged over 60 compared to 12% for all sectors in the UK.

It has been argued that as people get older they become risk adverse and that older managers and in this instance, owners might be less flexible Karami et al (2006). Prior research purports that age is inversely related to risk taking and also the view of what is risk i.e. taking a risk as opposed to taking a calculated risk through research and decision-making. Nowadays it is expected that younger managers are better educated as there are more opportunities However,, this research indicates that older managers are more likely to undertake alliances as experience is used to aid the decision making. Despite this assumption, it is revealed that younger managers are equally likely to carry out analysis that results in their seeking out alliances However,,, what is clear is that it is different stages of the process where they seek alliances. Research by Yordanova and Alexandrova-Boshnakova (2011) revealed that entrepreneurial types tend to be older which may explain the results found in this research.

For young managers of young firms the need for alliances for financial purposes are more prevalent as they have not yet progressed to market and are currently focused on either research and development or production. The more experienced managers were more likely to seek alliances for other reasons. As SMEs are considered flexible then it could also be reported that SMEs and not the managers are more risk tolerant. As introduced in chapters six and seven there was significant correlation between some of the demographics of respondents and pursuing strategic alliance These were experience and age. H_1 is accepted as there is significant correlation between a managers prior experiences and their willingness to form Strategic Alliances, furthermore there is a significant relationship between careful planning and success.

Managers in this study indicated their experience in terms of how long they had managed their business and also their engagement with alliances.

Results show there is correlation between a manager's experience and their willingness to engage in alliances. It is also identified that managers who are experienced are more likely to employ environmental scanning tools and experience achievement of goals. The findings in this study reveal similar characteristics to those found by Berry (1998) where managers use their prior experiences to make decisions and this can have an impact on future planning and in particular their engagement in alliances. Those who reported successful alliances also indicated that they would undertake further alliances while the majority indicated that strategic alliance planning and formation should be an integral part of their strategic management.

Dobbs and Hamilton (2007) posit that firms whose managers have had prior experience are less likely to make mistakes, for firms in this study this was possible as they worked towards aligning their strategies and there is support from Entrialgo (2002) who demonstrates that co alignment between characteristics and strategy has positive outcomes, therefore the result of this study comes as no surprise when the managers self report both a need to align their alliance strategy with the overall strategy and experience alliance success.

It has been argued that as people get older or indeed more experienced they become more risk adverse and that older more experienced managers may be less open to alliances, and whether an owner manager may be more cautious than a paid manager or CEO as they have more to lose if poor decision making and strategies are not carried out as intended resulting in poor firm's performance. Support comes from Dvir et al (2010) that it is difficult to empirically find evidence to demonstrate a causal relationship between manager's traits and success. While individuals characteristics do not alone influence decision making background characteristics such as managerial experience does have a significant impact on their decision making. In addition, to continue this paradox it is easy to see that age, which contributes to managerial experience, has a bearing on decision making. It is clear to see that when profiling the small business owner that it is useful to accept that on one hand certain variables do not directly influence others but when taken holistically one will impinge on others in a given situation. Research is contradictory as it does not soundly indicate that younger entrepreneurs are more innovative and ambitious (Dvir et al, 2010) this research showed positive correlation between a managers age, the firms age and their activities on all counts except for marketing suggesting that younger managers are more likely to be focused on product development than their market, this finds support from Lasch et al (2007) who also cite this product myopia on high failure rates. For all ages of the self reported data all managers in the high tech industry were highly educated with managers who were older also having more managerial experience and experience of strategic alliances.

Pansiri (2005) argues that choosing to embark on a strategic alliance is a reflection of managers characteristics and perceptions However,, the study considers the alliance holistically i.e. strategic alliance option, strategic alliance type and choice of strategic alliances partner this suggests a strategic management of the alliance therefore corroborating the evidence in this study that strategic decision making impacts on alliance formation. Furthermore Pansiri (2005 pp 1097) states

> "The assumptions behind this view are that first, strategic alliances are human constructs, designed out of decisions reached by managers in regard to how the organisation desires to deal with its environment. Secondly, that strategic alliances form a unique part of organizational strategy."

Findings from this research differ from that of Lau et al (2008 pp 772) who state

220

"The demographics of the top managers have no statistically significant effects on strategic orientation"

They also conclude that strategic orientation is also not related to firm's size. I conclude that the psychological not physiological characteristics that significantly effect decision making are important demographics However,,; their conclusion that strategic orientation is not related to firms size is not entirely conclusive because other factors can influence this. Prior managerial experience and management capabilities are more likely to be able to successfully predict success (Dvir. et al, 2010) as they discovered little correlation between personality traits and the ability to predict entrepreneurial success.

Support for this comes from (Cooper et al, 1994; Lasch et al, 2007) who show that the experience of the manager is a critical success factor confirming the findings in this research that while an individuals demographics alone do not significantly influence their decision to engage in or avoid alliances they are a critical success factor. It also finds support for Pansiri's assertion that for technology alliances age and education do have an impact on decision making as these are shaped by a persons experiences and will have a direct bearing on their understanding of the need for careful planning and once undertaken an alliance the need to monitor and evaluate it carefully.

These results confirms those of Sanyal and Guvenli (2004) that perceptions of managers can be generalised and applied across similar sectors. They were able to confirm that there are significant differences when the age, qualifications, gender etc are introduced as variables. While further support comes from Goll et al (2008) that there is significant correlation between management demographics and business strategy. This study finds evidence that managers are more likely to look for marketing alliances and that an individuals characteristics alone do not influence alliance decision making, rather their motivation for the alliance, past experiences and the identification in their own lack of capabilities or resources to conduct their business successfully. These findings are contradictory to "product myopia" in SMEs as suggested by Lasch et al (2007).

8.2.1.1.3 Education

A manager's education is likely to influence firms performance as a well educated manager are more likely to display innovative characteristics. Managers with extended education are likely to bring about increased firm's performance and results from this study show that managers are likely to be flexible in their approach but also display strategic management. However,, the younger managers who have less managerial experiences are able through their education to exploit available management tools to assist with planning Dobbs and Hamilton (2007), further more according to Herrmann et al (2006 p24)

> "knowledge gain in the past has a crucial influence on current and future research..." "Successful companies profit from their superior knowledge".

It is therefore hypothesised through research objective one that managers education is an important variable in strategic management and decision making and would play a part in the development and successful management of strategic alliances in particular to gain new knowledge and know how (Rogers, 2001)

In chapter six, it is suggested that younger managers were similarly highly educated but lacked managerial experience while for the older managers many had postgraduate degrees and considerable experience; this is considered the norm for high tech managers Rogers (2001).

Support comes from (Yahaya and Abu-Bakar, 2007: Dvir et al, 2010) that managers in the high tech are higher educated to a higher level than managers in other sectors. Green et al (1996) found significant differences between

222

characteristics between managers found in the high tech sector compared to those found in other sectors

Colombo and Grilli (2008) offer two ways in which education and experience can affect performance, those with higher education qualifications are assumed to be able to successfully manage a business and their higher educational attainment would be reflected in both their industry specific knowledge and their decision making abilities. Combining education and experience managers in the high tech industry are expected to be able to rise to the challenges of this fast paced industry turning threats into opportunities as well as being able to multi task at all the different job tasks faced by owner managers.

This study's findings receives support and corroborates those of other researchers that the manager is key to the success of the firm. The manager is charged with providing the culture, the vision and practices of the firm all highly influenced by their inherent characteristics. Others have concluded that management teams with a range of skills are an important factor in relation to the long term future growth of these SMEs for the resource strained smaller firm's this is a luxury avoided instead the manager uses his qualities to build relationships with other firms to obtain the resources and knowledge required to market their products. Previous research has linked that when a manager only focuses on the R&D of the firm's and ignores the market until it is required to access them then the business is constrained and survival threatened as it is not sufficient to have a good product the success lies in the introduction of said product into to the market and obtaining market share and thereby obtaining funding to continue with R&D.

Findings support the notion that decision making about strategic alliances is dependant on the characteristics of the manager and that motivations that come from either demographics or prior experience do influence their decision to engage in or avoid strategic alliances as an alternative to investing internally. Instead, these firms choose to combine their core capabilities with those of similarly placed firms for the benefit of both firms. This confirms the findings of Das and He (2006) that careful partner selection is important

223

However,,, it is noted that their empirical evidence was based on small firms seeking partnerships with larger firms.

There is evidence that alliances are favoured by SMEs to enable them to be more competitive and this brings the paradox of competition and cooperation many firms preferring this than competing in the same market with similar products. However,, there is significant evidence that successful mangers have particular characteristics in common and practice similar decision making strategies confirming that that individuals characteristics and prior experiences exert influence over their firms and if others emulate this behaviour they could if not design out failure totally but could minimise the risk as reported by Mitsuhashi (2002) whose study on a small number of firms offered guidelines However,, like many restricted studies it is not clear study whether it could be generalised across all sectors.

It is surmised that SMEs and in particular those in the high tech sector are not likely to be successful long term without the application of strategic management. This requires the mangers that are likely to be technically enabled to understand that their firm's is subject to external influences and must be managed to ensure growth. It is important that they recognise the need for strategic fit between their technology strategy i.e. their products and processes and their business strategy and marketing strategy.

As literature continues to search for a paradigm that can envelope SM in all its ambiguity research will continue to focus on the application rather than on the methods used. Stonehouse & Pemberton, (2002) argue that it is important that there is a distinction between strategic thinking, planning and execution and while Mintzberg advocates flexibility, it is important to plan not only where the business is going but also how it will cope with environmental uncertainty.

Support comes from Brinckmann et al (2010) whose findings confirms that "business planning increases the performance of both new and established small firms", However,, they agree that there are different factors that influence relationship strength, with support from Kakati (2003) that factors influence success or failure. Support for the view that long term strategies and business planning in turbulent environments comes from Goll et al (2008) who also support that a relationship between business strategy and firm's performance exists.

8.2.1.1.4   Management and strategy application

In studying management behaviour and in particular when choosing growth strategies such as alliances for whatever purpose and in any part of the process the role of the manager is always critical and in this respect this study has found consensus with existing literature. In particular the notion that SME owners are often scientists and start the firm's on the basis of their skill whether it is in software development, nano technology or in medicine rather than because they have any particular management or marketing ability or indeed identified any marketing opportunity for their proposed product or services. There is evidence in literature that owners of such firms tend to be visionaries and good leaders and this may explain some of their management ability.

Managers who use environmental analyse, SWOT and other scanning tools will then make decisions based on their findings whether or not they may benefit from alliances. The more proactive and formal planners amongst these managers have indicated that they would benefit from incorporating the strategic alliance planning into their overall business strategy. This suggests that these managers understand the industry they operate in and also their own capabilities and how to exploit them.

As well as the managers own capabilities it is reported that within the studied firms that most were able to recruit sufficient professional staff. This is confirmatory to other studies were the recruitment and retention of sufficient human resources of the right calibre is essential but some find limited due to the firms needs, location and the infancy of the firm's whose entrepreneurial characteristics may not be enough to lure competent workers. In addition, for this reason other studies show that firms have to look elsewhere for this resource, through correlation analysis, this study confirms that availability of the correct human resource enabled the firms to meet their objectives both financial and technological.

The data analysis suggests that firms have to have a certain level of experience to successfully form and manage alliances. Therefore, the assumption that managers' experience and demographics has a positive effect on successful alliance management is grounded and support for this is found in prior research.

In summary a firms resource capabilities in terms of management and human resource does have a significant impact on alliance formation and success. It is revealed However,,, that firm's size does have a significant impact on this. There is positive correlation between experience and alliances as experienced managers acknowledge the reduced costs incurred when working together.

It is reported in other studies that experienced firms can exploit their complementary resources and minimise risk to themselves. Firms learn by their own experience and if experienced firms practices are used as benchmarks for others then alliance formation is a practical solution for SMEs in the high tech sector.

However,, alliances are not without cost, these costs can not be recaptured and include time and effort and the allocation of valuable resources in setting up the alliance. The effective management of alliances requires practice and patience with the knowledge that resource acquisition or capability increase will benefit the firm. Many firms will be tempted by the acquisition of resources with limited expenditure However,, it is this lack of motivation and commitment that can lead to alliance failure. Managing the alliance is a challenge and managers have to be able to manage their own firm's and the hybrid even if it is only for a short time. Repeated partnering increases trust and can reduce costs significantly over time, management sees the lack of trust as factoring highly in the failure of their alliance.

8.2.1.1.5 Management perceptions and strategic alliance behaviour

Managers perceived that the biggest benefit from alliances were gaining market access and thereby reducing the competition, However,, reducing competitive pressure was ranked as least important. The younger firms considered obtaining financial assistance for research and development as a primary benefit for alliances. Logistics scored the least for this section with only 181 managers considering that they would benefit from assistance in this stage of the process. Market access is seen as the biggest motivator for cooperation and are perceived as being the biggest benefit from strategic alliances.

The motivations and perceived critical success factors are summarised briefly here in relation to management. The primary success factor for alliance was perceived by the managers to be mutual trust However,, it was also felt that being based in a cluster of similar firms would assist them through networking. Geographical proximity to a potential partner was considered least important to the managers. Critical success factors varied by industry However,,, mutual trust was perceived as being most important. Compatible management styles are considered more important than complementary resources as firms where managerial goals are compatible they may work together to obtain resources from another party, their relationship providing some credibility when approaching a third party.

The findings showed that managers perceive partners motivations for forming alliances as having a big impact on their success or failure. It is considered that careful strategic planning and management can reduce the risk of failure and result in successful alliances. It is identified in literature that firms look for ways to survive and therefore recognise the need for planning.

Together with motivation is the importance of compatible goals, aims and objectives and this was considered critical in the studied firms. The objectives of the firms involved in an alliance need to be the same However,, this study suggests that provided the outcomes are the same then the objectives if not identical need to create added value and to ensure that competitive advantage is obtained and maintained. Of those who had successful alliances the majority cited mutual trust as important in helping to maintain the relationship.

Therefore this study proposes that partnership objectives can be slightly different However,, the expected outcomes need to be the same and in alignment. Participating managers need to combine their firm's objectives and coordinate the resources they have to ensure they are complementary and that they are equally committed to the alliance. It can be expected that during each stage of the alliance compromises may need to be made However,, there should always be an element of win win for all partners and that compromise should not have the effect of negating the alliance and increasing the risk of failure or early termination. This suggests definite cooperation with very clear boundaries, identification of where resource limitation occur in both firms and if neither firm's has a particular resource that they work together to obtain it.

Flexibility is a key issue in alliances as not every possible eventuality can be covered in a document and therefore a partners ability to be flexible is seen as an intangible part of the contract in ensuring that the alliance works. These findings are subjective as the perception of the managers into the failure or success may depend on the outcome and could be early termination, lack of product development or did not realise immediate financial gain.

Those firms willing to consider alliances were predominately in the industries where there products or processes would be less likely to be imitated or if imitated they would have the market share until the imitators followed. Those who thought that they might lose control or ownership of their firm or not be able to control their alliance were justified in their fear as almost 50% of those who engaged in an alliance perceived it as a failure. These firms had a tendency to have undertaken a large numbers of alliances and an important feature would be to see their performance over time soothing this study is not able to perform. For these firms there strategic planning was examined at length and it was seen that these firms did not consider planning important in the following areas, in the interpretation for this section some suggestions are considered.

Findings show that managers do not consider that they reduce competitive pressures when they form alliances indeed they perceive that they lose control of the firm's However,, only 52% who felt this actually had experienced alliance failure with the other 48% reporting success in their alliances and for many who indicate this have performed badly in the alliance arena.

In technology and software development there is a propensity towards alliances However,, these findings show over 50% perceived failure rate. This failure rate is replicated across many of the sectors with only the gaming technology a fairly new concept showing a 100% failure rate. The high failure rate are consistent with other research findings and exploration of the reasons for failure reveal many permutations of the causes.

Analysing the planning behaviour of the managers showed that the studied firms considered alliances as a long term strategy and were not considering them for quick financial gain. The majority were willing to seek alliances in the areas they felt less competent with the majority looking for financial or marketing assistance. The strategy formulation avoidance which is seen in a large number of the participant firms confirms literature that those firms who work in innovative environments and in what are considered high growth areas are not planners However,, this does not mean that they do not plan informally or acknowledge that they will need to plan at some stage in their life cycle. To conclude firms who employ strategic management techniques perform better than those who do not in the long term.

Results from the study reveal that managers who reported that they did not think it necessary to employ strategic management techniques reported their financial performance and objectives to be met equally well as those who actively carried out extensive environmental and competitor analysis. Firms who reported the highest sales figures also report that the technical objectives of the company are met.

Existing literature proposes that managers play an active role in the development of strategy and in this study it is clear that those managers who perceive strategic management as important strive to ensure that it is consistent throughout the firms activities. Again this will be influenced drastically by the attitude, perceptions and prior experience of the manager, there is some evidence in literature where it is discussed that the firm's as a unit of analysis is behaving in a certain way when the firm's is being controlled by an individual with thoughts and actions that impact on the decision making. Conversely there are equal amounts of literature that provide empirical evidence that small firms do not practice strategic management and as a result find themselves having to revolutionise their organisation in response to internal or external factors, which can put the firm's into crisis.

Some of the evidence in this study contradicts existing research results in that other authors have concluded that not engaging in formal strategic decision making and application of tools and techniques does not necessarily affect the performance of small firms. In light of this those firms in this study who reported achieving high sales did not provide any other financial data for example the cost of these sales in production and marketing.

It could also be deduced when taking age of the firms into account that the planning has evolved over the life of the business hence older firms report actively employing strategic management techniques which contribute to firm's performance.

Results confirms that managers who carry out strategic management and planning will be in a position to control alliances or other relationships it engages in. Those firms who indicated they had experienced successful alliances also reported that they carried out strategic planning. Business trend analysis was the least used technique However,, industry and competitor analysis were considered important by the firms. 57% of those who had successful alliances considered it important to integrate the alliances into the overall strategy of the firm's.

8.2.1.1.6 Managers perceptions of critical success factors in alliance formation

The critical success factors as perceived by managers as contributing to successful alliance formation and management will be based on their own skills, education and prior experience. The critical success factors will be discussed further in 8.3. The characteristics that most influence the decision making are managerial experience and age of the manager. There is no statistical difference in the adoption of strategic management between the genders and it is considered that SME owners are likely to replicate successful practices of other firms benchmarked against all industrial sectors and not just in the high tech sector, particularly women are identified in the service sector as formal strategists.

Managerial characteristics as an influence on decision making are widely researched and this study has confirmed that this is justified. Results are confirmatory to the incumbent literature that managers individuality and the perceptions generated by this individuality will reflect on their management decision making.

The findings in this study reveal similar characteristics to those found by Berry (1998) where managers use their prior experiences to make decisions and this can have an impact on future planning and in particular their engagement in alliances. Those who reported successful alliances also indicated that they would undertake further alliances while the majority indicated that strategic alliance planning and formation should be an integral part of their strategic management.

The relationship that an owner manager has with his firm's is one of the main differences between them and larger firms. They exercise a high level of control over the business (Dobbs and Hamilton, 2007) and therefore the characteristics of the owner manager is likely to have a large influence over the performance of the firm's and the decision to form alliances or to go it alone. According to Dobbs and Hamilton (2007) the building of an identikit of a SME owner is an important step in business research and for this reason profiles of mangers were established in chapter six. Furthermore they claim that the characteristics of the manager have minimal influence on the firm's However,, for this study analysis shows that these variables do have some effect and coupled with their strategic planning intentions have a significant influence on their propensity to form strategic alliances..

8.2.2 Research objective 2

To investigate the relationship between demographics and background characteristics of firms and strategic alliance success.

Proposition 2 Identify key demographics and background characteristics of the firms to establish the relationship between firm's demographics and strategic alliance success. These demographics and background characteristics include Firm's age, size, industry type and their strategy.

Table 8.2 Hypothesis two

Hypothesis	Outcome
H_2 There is significant correlation between firms demographics and background characteristics and successful strategic alliances	Hypothesis two is strongly supported by the firm's size and age.

8.2.2.1   Discussion for research objective two – hypothesis two

The following section discusses the findings for hypothesis two. The outcomes are discussed in relation to existing literature and research and identifies confirmation of results or explains the differences.

Despite prior perception that SMEs in the in the high tech sector do not engage in strategic management nor strategic alliances, this study has found that those who engage in strategic management are likely to form alliances as a strategic option for growth. How these collaborations are perceived may differ for example specific contracts with suppliers or customers may be perceived as a strategic alliance especially when supported by strategic management, it is argued by some for example Xie and Johston (2004) that while all Strategic Alliances can be assumed to be inter firm's collaborations, definitions of Strategic Alliances means that not all inter firm's collaborations are Strategic Alliances. According to Varadarajan and Jayachandran (1999) to be a Strategic alliance they must be seeking and achieving a sustainable competitive advantage and from the findings in this study it can be seen that those firms who have engaged in alliances have done so to achieve competitive advantage.

Findings from this study corroborate with the literature that there are a number of significant correlations between the size of the company and its propensity towards strategic management. SME owners recognise that employment of business tools can increase the performance of the business and will therefore whether formal or informal planners will employ the tools they perceive necessary, indeed findings from this study indicate that the firms will cherry pick the ones that will best assist them for example in the gaming industry which is a relatively new sector in terms of online gambling etc do not use industry analysis but look at wider environmental issues. Corroboration comes from Small bone et al (1995) that there is not single type of strategy that ensures growth However,, it is agreed with Kraus et al (2006) that formal planning has a significant impact on firms performance also see Porter (2000).

8.2.2.2   Age of the respondent firms

Developing the research questions for this study it was suggested that the respondents in this study would reveal that the older the firm's the more likely they would be to instigate formal strategic planning, However,, it is clear from the results that there is significant use of strategic management from inception (γ = ¯.063, p < 0.01). As well as indicating that strategic planning was important to the firms it was also indicated that strategic alliances should be combined with the strategy of the firm's.

The high tech sector is viewed as high growth sector and therefore it is relevant to look at other high growth studies as research on SMEs in the high tech sector and alliance success is scarce (Drago, 1997). "High growth firms have often been referred to as 'gazelles' although the term is now increasingly taken to refer only to young, and usually small, high growth enterprises. The OECD defines gazelles as "the subset of high-growth enterprises which are up to five years old" BERR (2008).

Research into strategic alliance formation and success has tended to focus on larger older firms that are considered MNEs. Success of small businesses that relate to strategic alliances and in particular those in the high tech sector appear to be grouped with entrepreneurial studies. Das and He (2006) define these However,, others who have researched small businesses in the high tech sector have not.

"entrepreneurial firms are generally young, small and

highly innovative firms in industries with rapidly developing technologies. (Das and He 2006 pp 120)

These firms are also called new high tech ventures relating to their young age March and Gunasekaran (1999). Das and He (2006) reviewed the differences between what they called entrepreneurial firms i.e. new start ups and established firms. They considered the setting up of alliances between the two types of firms recognising the inequality of power that would exist. Das and He (2006 pp 115) provide support that despite prior research

236

stressing how larger, older firms are likely to be more innovative due to the resources available for R&D, that younger firms are just as innovative and due to less complex organisational set ups are flexible to engage in innovation.

"small firms have been found to have higher rates of innovation compared to their share of sales or number of employees.."

Support for this comes from Shefer and Frenkel (2005) who found that firm's age and size could affect investment in R&D and had a significant negative effect on the extent of R&D activity of the firm's. They also support findings in this research that older firms may be able to acquire investment for research and development more easily than younger firms due to having established a reputation However,, younger firms are more likely to reinvest as their operating costs due to size are less, what is clear is that younger firms do have the capability to engage in R&D activities and if necessary seek collaboration to do so.

Smallbone et al (1995) found that age or maturity of the firm's was not related to its ability to grow, this is contradictory to this study where young SMEs were equally likely to search for strategic alliances as older firms However,, the reasons for doing so were different BERR (2008). The age of the company is an important demographic as young companies may not be able to attract investment and therefore not survive. On the other hand young successful companies may be easy targets for larger competitors who seek to take advantage of innovative capacity and who offer experience in exchange.

The age of the company combined with the age of the manager was seen as an important factor when considering alliances as a young firm's with an experienced manager may be able to negotiate, implement and manage an alliance for the benefit of the firm's whereas a younger inexperienced manager may fall prey to a larger firm's seeking to obtain innovative capacity through alliance with a young innovative firm's but who may not deliver its side of the agreement, this phenomena of partnering success has been widely researched for example (Mitsuhashi, 2002; Mandal et al, 2003; Pansiri, 2005; Das and He, 2006; Sarkis et al, 2007; Dealtry, 2008; Teng and Das, 2008; Dodourova, 2009; Gulati et al, 2009; Das and Kumar, 2010)

It is observed that most of the sample firms are either very young and in their set up stage and are currently very innovative or are older well established companies who have accumulated a substantial amount of experience. For this survey the age distribution is positively skewed with most of the SMEs being in their infancy. The majority of firms (63%) being considered in their infancy i.e. under ten years of age were also classified as micro firms due to the low number of employees. The less mature firms were focused on a strategy that was to target a broad marekt and concentrating on product differentiation. According to Lau et al (2008) firm's age is usually a reflection of its resources and its ability to be competitive However,, they also report that for young firms simply investing in human resources and R&D of firms is not sufficient, due to their resource strained position they will need to embark on strategic alliances, further to this many others also view the need for alliances, the understanding of the motivations and the processes of R&D when working with others for example during the setting up of consortia for R&D so that multiple firms work together rather than the previously studied dyadic alliances (Eisner et al, 2009).

From research by Delmar et al (2003) The age of the firm's was significantly related to cluster membership However,, from this study younger firms were tended to be stand alone while the more mature firms were situated in the clusters and relied on them for marketing purposes.

The literature confirms that young firms will seek strategic alliances as they are critical to their success as they enable them to access resources and capabilities from other firms with little cost (Beverland and Bretherton, 2001; Chen and Karami, 2010. A defining feature of younger businesses controlled by a younger manager is that they lack the competency to develop and control a succesful alliances.

However,, through empirical research in this study and the review of incumbent literature it can be seen that a firms age may significantly impact on strategic alliance performance with an understanding that firms of a different age will look for alliances at different stages and for different reasons. Further support for this observation comes from Dobbs and Hamilton (2007) In their findings that young firms could grow rapidly if they were able to acquire resources and capabilites which would enable them to reduce the effect of environmental changes and to meet market demand. For the firms in this study there was a strong correlation between age and investment for research and development ($\gamma = .140*$ p $> .0.5$).

Analysing the figures further it was seen that younger firms are able to attract investment However,, while older firms were less able the amount that they did secure were higher. A quarter of all firms under ten years of age had attracted up to £50,000 investment and although not investigated may have come from busines start up and other grants.

8.2.2.3   Size of the respondent firms

There has been a high rise in the number of SMEs in the high tech sector in recent decades and the study of these have provided important evidence in the contribution of SMEs to the economy and the contribution to job and wealth creation and have inspired further research from academia and interest from policy makers and practitioners for example see (Hoffman et al, 1998; March and Gunasekaran, 1999; Porter, 2000; Jocumsen, 2002; Das and He, 2007; Dobbs and Hamilton, 2007; Karami, 2007; Lau et al, 2008; Haeussler et al, 2010).

The European classification for SMEs size by number of employees has been used for this study with the majority of the firms being classified as micro. Analysis from this study reveal that over 60% of studied firms had less than five employees with a further 35.5% having up to 10 employees, only 4.8% of the firms reported having over 100 employees.

Hagedoorn and Schakenraad (1994) put forward empirical evidence that for small firms the barriers to engaging in alliances may be high and found;

"no general significant direct effects of size.." and "different types of industries show divergent relations between size and innovation" Hagedoorn and Schakenraad (1994 pp 300)

these results differ to those of this survey which show that the SMEs were able to engage in alliances which may reflect the current economic climate where all firms are needing to obtain resources externally than securing their own resources through internal expansion and that as manages in the firms are more able to recruit and retain expert employees their ability to innovate increases as does their ability to forge strategic alliances and also conforming to literature that strategic alliances make sense for example see (Vyas et al, 1995; Berry, 1996; Drago, 1997; Berry and Taggart, 1998; Parker, 2000; Pegals and Yang, 2000; Beverland and Bretherton, 2001; Hagedoorn and Duysters, 2002; Clarke-Hill et al, 2003; Ju et al, 2005; Dealtry, 2008; Gravier et al, 2008; Teng and Das, 2008; Dodourova, 2009; Gulati et al, 2009; Chen

240

and Karami, 2010; Haeussler et al, 2010; Srivastava and Frankwick, 2011). This survey also found that within particular sectors the propensity to form strategic alliances was higher than in others, these tended to be where investment costs were higher. Further interesting correlations were found between size and the participation and success of the alliances. Size did not have a significant effect on whether or not a firm has had experience of alliances, However,, it did have significant correlation on multiple experience of alliances with a high correlation between experience and success. Multiple experiences (γ = .435** p = > 0.01) and success (γ = .316** p = > 0.01). When correlated with the age of the owner these figures were still significant, there was a significant correlation between the age of the manager and alliance success (γ = .167* p = > 0.05). This suggests that as a firm's grows it is able to manage alliances more effectively and have the resource and capabilities that make them attractive to partner firms, which may not be present in younger firms, and for this reason there is support from Hagedoorn and Schakenraad (1994)

".....intensity of strategic partnering tends to Rise with the increasing size of companies..... Firm size reflects the degree to which firms actively seek and find external opportunities in

strategic linkages" Hagedoorn and Schakenraad (1994 pp 302-303)

These are further supported by Berry (1996) as she suggests that as organisations grows they develop an external strategic orientation and for this reason may search for partners with complementary resources similar findings were reported by Mellat-Parast and Digman (2007).

As employees are the measurement of firm size it is important to look at the relevance of employees and their role in the success of the strategic alliance. It is expected that for these firms that the management style is one of participation making it easier for firms to recruit and retain top specialists in their field. The firms in this study invested in their employees and also reinvested in the firm's confirming that firms with . high level of R&D need to attract employees with these specialised skills. These firms who plan to reinvest also indicated that they employ strategic management techniques, there is some correlation between the size of the business and these findings.

241

The number of employees significantly impact on the success of alliances, which suggests that having the right personnel can help a firms performance. Using the size of the organisation rather than its age as an indicator of growth has helped to identify that SMEs do not develop incrementally but will progress and stagnate as changes occur in the business.

Herrmann et al (2006) reported that the size of a company does not have a significant influence on the creation of radical innovation and indeed this research is confirmatory as regardless of size the companies self reported as having numerous products at different stages as well as engaging in research and development, However,, the size of the firm's are correlated to the strategic alliance success of the firm's.

8.2.2.4 Investment, productivity and alliance success of respondent SMEs

The high levels of investment internally and from external sources suggest that for successful SMEs in the high tech sector R&D is key to obtaining dominance in their niche market. While there are many examples in literature where R&D and product development is the focus of alliance strategy and in particular how this reflects on the capabilities of the firms for example see (Parker, 2000; Pegels and Young, 2000; Haeussler et al, 2010) for the studied firms external collaborative R&D is not the prime focus as suspected instead the focus is on the markets and gaining customer access.

There is some collaboration with Porter whereby firms form interrelationships in the value chain of their firm's with another to gain competitive advantage. This research has highlighted that marketing is the most sought after relationship as more firms choose cooperation over competition. According to Smallbone et al (1995) and their empirical research in to high growth firms generally and not aimed at high tech identified characteristics of the firm's which were consistent with the findings of this research. They stated that firms could not be led by their production but had to have market development strategy in place. They identified the important role of the manager or as they termed it the leader in controlling the whole process and not just being a factory manager.

The difference between their research and this study was that it was longitudinal and covered a range of non tech, low and high tech firms and they concentrated on the growth factor although they corroborate the need for managers to be proactive and form strategies that encompass all areas of the business for long term growth this notion is also supported by Ju et al (2005).

Managers of SMEs must adopt not only managerial skills and tools as the firms grows and their products are ready for consumption and marketing imperatives become dominant but must also begin to have strategy as its underlying philosophy. Determinants of success for the business is when a technical or scientific proficient manager also gains proficiency in developing long term growth strategies which match the "innovativeness" of the firm's with clear market strategy. This helps to improve the firms ability to establish partnerships and engage in successful strategic alliances. Literature shows that this can only be achieved where a strong strategic orientation is developed and where all activities from research and development stage are controlled, directed and integrated by effective strategic management as extensively researched and studies for example see (Berry, 1996; Berry and Taggart, 1998; March and Gunaskearan, 1999; O'Regan and Ghobadian, 2002; Ju et al, 2005; Garengo and Bititci, 2007; Lau et al, 2007; Dodourova, 2009; Grawe et al, 2009). The responses in this study regarding sales were low and not validated and finds support from Gulati (1998) that researchers should avoid using traditional accounting and financial measures when considering the success of an alliance as long term relationships are not always measurable, support also comes from Kraus et al (2006 pp 339) who champion employee numbers as an indicator of growth for the following reasons

"First, financial data are reported to be unreliable in the context of small and young firms.

Second, growth is an important goal for small and young firms, and third, employment growth is a more stable indicator than turnover growth, since firms only add employees when a higher level of business volume is likely to be stabilized in the future"

8.2.2.5   Firm's capabilities

Despite prior research that finds that SMEs are unlikely to form successful alliances as they do not have the knowledge to take proactive steps Minshall et al (2008) to form strategic alliances often becoming the subject of crisis management Herbane (2010).   The empirical research from this study suggests that for SMEs who remain resource poor and reliant on their core capabilities are recognising the need to cooperate and that the higher education level and prior experiences of these managers means they exploit their own core capabilities and acquire resources and capabilities from others to if not grow then certainly to remain stable and profitable (Byast and Karami, 2010).

A firm's may have many capabilities and resources but they may not lead to superior performance or growth of a firm's if they offer no opportunities for exploitation or have no value outside the firm's. The studied firms self-reported that they were able to manage their resources and achieve organisational goals through their own capabilities and resourcefulness using external relationships where this was not achievable. For example some of

244

the firms are market aware and recognise the need to exploit their capabilities in providing what the consumer requires for some specialist firms this means relinquishing their own preferred specialisation for a more market driven activity. The skills of the individual managers are unique inside that firm's However,, many will be replicated by other managers but for those who can exploit their uniqueness then others may seek to work with them to take advantage of this capability possibly a scarce resource not readily available. This gives these firms a competitive advantage. Therefore it is important that managers recognise the assets it has in both tangible and intangibles. By aggregating the responses the following resources are seen as being owned by the SMEs in this study, corporate know how, employee specialisation, management capabilities and experience and an ability to locate resources and capabilities not readily available from within.

While they do not have departments in the form of HRM, marketing and financial accountants they still recognise the importance of these for the sustainability of the firm's and indeed many search for alliances to increase their own capabilities or invest in these areas.

Research by Ju et al (2005) investigated how a firms capabilities are factors in successful alliances, in this research the studied managers are identified as the firms resource and its capabilities are established through the demographics and background characteristics of the manager. It is clear from the data collection that the difference in managers age and experience are identified when they self report to being experienced or inexperienced and having certain capabilities. There is significant correlation between a managers age (γ= .627** p>0.01) and experience and their willingness and motivation towards forming strategic alliances. Resource constrained SMEs put a lot of onus on the manager to be able to strategically manage and plan the firms activities.

The fact that firms increase their propensity to form alliance with management experience suggests that managers rely on prior experience to assist with the formation of alliance. A firms strategy that is based on a managers experience will include long term planning, an experienced manger will be able to identify where it requires compatible assistance from and will be able to identify partners in advance rather than choose the wrong partner due to necessity Herbane (2010). Core competencies of a company have been significantly researched and in particular to their relationship in enabling the competitive advantages of a company to be exploited (Prahalad and Hamel, 1990; Herrmann et al, 2006).

8.2.2.6   Firm's activity and alliance

When the research questions were being developed the importance of the motives for seeking, developing and maintaining a strategic alliance for the firms were considered. In particular; was it the demographics of the owner? The literature review revealed the scarcity of research in this area and instead focused on reasons for failure, types of alliances and the merits of each. Berry and Taggart (1998) reported that it was important that all strategies of a firm's should be combined. Chapters six and seven of this study revealed that despite other research that strategic planning was considered important for high tech companies and adequate planning should also lead to strategic alliances.

As initial research in this study showed that SMEs did not fully conform to the expectations in literature with regard to their characteristics and motivations for alliances. To understand this further firms were asked to indicate at what stages in their process would they seek an alliance, this is because for SMEs it was felt that they may seek alliances for all the areas they had weaknesses with lack of experience not enabling them to have their alliance plan within their overall strategy so that at each stage of their process they would have the required assistance. The results showed that these firms did not consider alliances at any time during the initial research or business planning stage.

During the research and development stage there is strong correlation between firms looking for finance for their research and development and undertaking alliances for technology transfer as discussed in other studies for example see (Parker, 2005; Ju et al, 2005; Eisner et al, 2009). As identified above these firms also look for alliances where they can increase their knowledge and learning for without an increase in knowledge the alliance may not serve its purpose (Srivastava and Frankwich, 2011). Some of the firms who self reported will not have the same stages in their processes as others and for this reason the study reveals some results, which have to be taken with caution for example those who undertake clinical trials need customer access but at the time of reporting were not considering market access.

For the firms who need patents they will consider alliances throughout their pipeline, it is assumed that they approach these with caution as their product may be of a sensitive nature if they wish to protect it with a patent i.e. a new brand which does not want generic brands to be leaked onto the market before they have become the market leader. For those firms who are market led gaining access to new customers is a priority when forming alliances. The results from this study show that there is no significant correlation between the stage at which a firm's might seek an alliance and success ($\gamma = .087$ p = > 0.01).

8.2.2.7 Experienced and inexperienced firms

The data analysis undertaken in chapters six and seven demonstrates that the primary motives for inexperienced firms differ slightly from experienced firms with both identifying the need to seek assistance for market access. As SME high tech firms are generally resource poor the identification of these inexperienced firms that they would need to require external resources such as technical and management expertise through knowledge transfer.

Financial and expert assistance were seen as less important by the more experienced firms than by the inexperienced firms. There may be two reasons for this as more experienced firms have learnt that it is rare to obtain finance through strategic alliances and depend on their finance from other sources, the other is that prior experience has led the firms to be reluctant in sharing knowledge which may be exploited. The need for financial and managerial input varies between sectors with those in technology development being less reliant than those in pharmaceutical firms. The primary motives chosen by these firms indicates that their propensity to form strategic alliances and the reasons for choosing to do so suggest that the firms stage of growth and growth strategy is related to its cooperative activity.

The majority of the managers of experienced firms stated that they instigate the alliance themselves with a minority saying they had used a consultant, through correlation analysis it was seen that the use of a consultant did not affect the success of the alliance.

Market access was the prominent determinant for engaging in alliances for all firms while the younger firms also emphasised the importance of alliances for financing their research and development, requiring both technology and knowledge transfer from the relationships.

It was considered that managers needed to be flexible and to have compatible management styles as well as being resource complementary to enable alliances to be successful. The majority of the respondent firms indicated that they were experienced in terms of having engaged in alliances (n=228 56.7%). Of these it was thought that a profile of the characteristics required in a prospective partner was beneficial (n=137 42%) There was a strong negative correlation between the business strategy of the firm's and the success of the strategic alliance (γ = -.144** p = > 0.01). For those who created a profile of their proposed partner as part of their business strategy there was strong correlation between creating the profile and strategic alliance success (γ = .416** p = > 0.01). This confirms that forming a business strategy that was either formal or informal was beneficial to the firm's.

8.2.2.8   Motivations for entering alliances by surveyed firms

Seminal literature has been on the increase in service industries (Byast and Karami, 2009) and it would appear that there has been a servicing growth within the high tech industries. McIvor (2000) asserts that organisations are moving away from outsourcing such as security to outsourcing of key elements for example components manufacturing, logistics, design and R&D to the complete production and assembly resulting in some firms becoming experts in coordinating rather than production (Busi and McIvor, 2008). It is clear from prior research that to exploit its core capabilities a firm's should invest in activities where it is competent and outsource the rest, this view differs from those who champion strategic alliances where both firms exchange their capabilities for mutual benefit. The question this research requires answered is that if it is easier to outsource what motivates a manager to seek out implement, manage and monitor a strategic alliance. The results of this empirical study reveals that the motivation for entering alliances for the majority of respondents was to gain access to markets in particular new ones where they have no prior experience. They seek relationships with firms who have complementary resources and who seek similar benefits from the relationship.

Findings reveal that those who engage or perceive that others are motivated by a quick profit do not appear to have successful alliances and when qualitative analysis is carried out for their responses to all questions it can be seen that they do not view alliances as long term plans and often show significant shortcomings in their overall business practices failing to meet employee or customer satisfaction as they are motivated by production and profit and not driven by market demands, thus confirming that firms need to be market driven.

This study has shown that a significant number of the firms will move between a strategy based on their technological ability and market needs as the company ages and their processes mature. Findings confirms the literature that the decision to focus on a particular strategy will be dependant on the growth stage of the business. Therefore motivation for forming alliances will be dependant on the level of technological maturity of the firms products and where they need the alliance as per Wisnieski and Soni (2004).

For each alliance that is formed there will be a number of factors which influence the motivation for entering the alliance. This will include whether or not the alliance was part of the long term planning and strategic management of the company or a cry for help, a cry for help may alert predatory firms to the possibility of a takeover while a firm's that has strategic management in place and has planned for the alliance will find themselves in a more powerful place from which to negotiate terms and conditions.

There is evidence that firms have to ensure that for an alliance to work certain assumptions are based around knowing the partner and the industrial sector. Results from this survey indicate that both partners need to recognise the role of the partnering firm's and that there must be flexibility and mutual trust between the partners to contribute to the alliance success. Managers are positively motivated towards success of the alliances and strive to seek out complementary partners through profiling.

As well as understanding each other's motivations there are other factors that both partners recognise;-

- awareness of the technical and financial reputation of the other firm's and they believe that they can contribute what they have stated and will keep to the alliance in terms of resources offered and commitment.

- Recognition that the alliance is a partnership born out of the recognition that the firms while their objectives may differ slightly that their resources are complementary and that together they can expel inherent weaknesses and promote strengths.
- Responsibilities for aspects of the alliance are understood and if not equally divided the rational for this is fully understood and agreed.

- Each partner can reasonably expect the same gain from the alliance unless mutually agreed prior to commencing the alliance.

- Mutual trust is evident and that both firms work to create a relationship and neither acts in a predatory way.

- Clauses are built in to prevent damaging behaviour.

These results confirms work by Lorange and Roos (1991) that it is important to ensure the strategic fit of the alliance prior to commencement.

8.2.2.9   Industrial sector

Prior research into alliance behaviour of SMEs while scarce is still evident and chooses to focus on a single industry pharmaceutical for example Casper and Matraves (2003) and in the area of ICT and software development Lasch et al (2007) or aerospace, Smith (2003) and does not look at differences within this industry itself as a result it was considered for the purpose of this research to consider the industry sector of the SMEs.

As there are few studies (Jones-Evans and Westhead, 1996; Rogers, 2001) with which to compare this research directly due to the dyadic nature of prior research.   This research considered the exploration of industry type in relation to hypothesis two as important as this may have identified differences and similarities of micro firms in the high tech sector who may behave differently to their larger counterparts who are the subject for individual study. For example SMEs may be carrying out research or design work which larger firms are outsourcing as they can longer be competitive if they carry out this work in house. As discussed elsewhere outsourcing for larger firms to SMEs is growing in popularity with both practitioners as a way to reducing costs and academics as a unit of study. Re factoring the variable how many of your alliances were a success to indicate 1= success 2= not considered a success the findings from this survey reveal that there is no significant correlation between the industry sector the firm's consider themselves to be operating in and experiencing strategic alliance success (γ = ‾.014, p < 0.01) these results were a little surprising as it was considered that industry sector would influence alliance success. As literature singles out in particular pharmaceutical firms these were cross tabbed with alliance success but still did not reveal a correlation between industry and alliance success therefore it is thought that for those who report alliance success there are more factors impacting on this than industry sector.

8.3   Alliance success factors for the 21st Century

Work by Das and He (2006) focused on alliances between entrepreneurial firms and established firms their findings included the not surprising result that little work had been undertaken into the alliance behaviour of the young SMEs and how little guidance there is for these firms, to help fill that gap and in view of the importance of strategic alliances in the future of small high tech firms the following guidelines have been adopted using prior suggestions from Gomes-Casseres (1998) and Mitsuhashi (2002) and the empirical research from this study.

- Strategic alliances need to be aligned with the firms overall strategy.
- They are a tool and like any other business tools must be employed and managed correctly.
- Take time to find a partner whose personal and business views and goals are compatible and who have complementary capabilities to offer.
- Ensure that a 'specialist' is appointed for each stage of the alliance, ensure that job tasks are fitted to that persons ability.
- Create trade offs for cooperation particularly where a prospective partner was/is also a competitor.
- Minimise conflict, have resolutions built into the alliance.
- Communication is important at all levels and all stages – keep it open communication develops trust.
- Ensure each partner employs an open door policy, if certain elements of the business are not to form part of the alliance ensure this is in the agreement, ensure that personnel from all firms are aware of what is going on otherwise distrust might develop.
- Alliances are long term relationships once this is understood it is easier to reduce short term expectations such as quick financial gains.
- Use the partners for further projects, multiple projects will reduce any negative aspects of short term problems in one project.
- Flexibility is key, business environments are changeable and firms need to allow the alliance to evolve and to take on board new opportunities.

The empirical findings from this study indicate that the surveyed firms are aware of the importance of mutual trust and commitment from the alliance partners and while it is generally accepted that this can be expected research from Das and He (2006) advises that while some personnel may deliberately work against an alliance for example if it feels that it poses a threat for example

> "an alliance with an entrepreneurial firm's with superior technologies and product development potentials will be

welcomed by the top management and the marketing department but will pose a threat to the internal research personnel". Das and He (2006 pp.125)

8.4 Chapter summary

This chapter has discussed the findings from the postal survey used to collect data from SMEs in the high tech sector in the UK. The data was analysed in chapters six and seven. The research questions have been answered and their associated hypothesis have been tested and the results have been discussed in 8.2 and 8.3. This chapter was divided into three sections. The first section introduced the chapter and discussed the variables chosen based on prior models used in management research.

Section two reviewed the research question, the research objective and the related hypothesis to be tested presenting the results synthesis it with prior research and providing interpretation for the results focussing on demographics and strategic planning of mangers and their firms in the high tech sector in the UK.

The presented and discussed data emphasises the importance of strategic management throughout the life cycle of both the firm's and its products. Commitment of the manager towards any undertaking is considered important while their experience is paramount in seeking strategic alliances and managing them.

Chapter Nine: Conclusions

9.1 Introduction

This book set out to examine (1) the factors of an owner manager's demographics and background characteristics that influence an owner manager's motivation for engaging in strategic alliances and thereby experiencing improved firm performance. (2) the market orientation of the firm, its strategic management preferences that contribute towards successful strategic alliances and improved firm performance.

The study was based on SMEs in the high tech industry and was underpinned by the theory of the researcher that if a firm undertook strategic management and planning then strategic alliances were a natural process for strategic growth for resource strained firms whose core capabilities were grounded in their scientific know how and not in business management.

The research was founded on the idea that when firms identified early in their operation that they lacked some core competencies or were under resourced and were able to accrue these through formally managing a business relationship then careful selection of the proposed partner and management of the partnership from a basis of mutual trust and common goals then firm objectives could be achieved.

In chapter one an introduction to the topic of strategic management and in particular alliance formation was introduced. This chapter outlined the research propositions, and highlighted some questions that had arisen through literature review. Chapter two examined the incumbent theory on strategic management, alliances providing to provide a definitive example of the terms used to explain management, strategic management and alliance behaviour during this book. Chapter three Presented the literature review using historical and contemporary literature to explore existing theories on management and alliances. Chapter four developed and presented the conceptual framework identifying key variables by synthesis the literature discussed in chapters two and three. Chapter five describes the research methodology from research design to data analysis. Chapter six provided descriptive analysis of the data. Presenting the data in a combination of tables, graphs and description each key theme of the book was presented. Chapter seven used statistical analysis to test the hypothesis and find relationships between the variables. Chapter eight introduces the findings in connection with the research propositions and discusses them using existing theory to support or explain the findings.

This final chapter reviews the theoretical contributions of the research with respect to the existing theory. Implications for practitioner, policy makers and academic are discussed. The limitations of the study are discussed with some suggestions for future research. Finally the major findings are represented together with their associated hypothesis.

9.2   Major findings

The main research questions of this empirical study were (1) How do management and firm demographics affect strategic alliance success in the high tech sector? and (2) What are the factors associated with strategic management of alliances in high tech sector? For the rest of this chapter the major findings in answer to the research questions will be discussed. The main outcome expectation of this research was a positive identification of the use of strategic management by the firms which resulted in choosing strategic alliances as an option for strategic growth gained by successful management of the strategic alliance as part of the overall management strategy which ultimately delivers improved firm performance.

Proposition One Identify key demographics of owner managers including gender, age, education and managerial experience to establish the affect that these demographics and background characteristics may have on alliance success. Identify key demographics of the studied firms to establish the relationship between firms demographics and strategic alliance success, these demographics include age, size, experience and the life cycle of the firm.

H_1 There is significant correlation between demographics and background characteristics of managers and strategic alliance success.

9.2.1 Management demographics

Both the managers and the studied firms display both homogeneity and heterogeneity. Homogeneity is indicated by the manager's age, educational levels and managerial experience and the motivation and support displayed by the managers for the formation of strategic alliances. Homogeneity is displayed by the firms age, size and innovative practices of the SMEs together with their propensity towards investment both internally and seeking external assistance when required. Heterogeneity comes from the variety of industries under the classification of High Technology firms, the diverse experiences of the managers, the diversity in product and firm stages of life cycles, the ability to attract and retain employees together with their perceptions of critical success factors for strategic alliances.

- Findings indicate that SMEs do use strategic management but do not always subscribe to prescriptive models of theoretical behaviour found in established manufacturing and production industries. They prefer to exploit their heterogeneity and remain flexible during the early stages of their life cycle.

- The research shows that owners find that they are successful and reach their financial objectives through using environmental scanning. For example businesses have reached their financial objectives through combining PESTEL analysis and customer service.

- Demographics and background characteristics of managers affect firm behaviour and performance.

- The educational attainment of the business owners has impacted on the strategic awareness and implementation methods of the owners.

- In particular education, age and experience have significant impact on how a firm is managed.

- Managers are motivated towards and involved in the strategic management of both the firm and strategic alliances.

- The findings in this study have provided another extension to the upper echelon theory by reporting that in firms where there is only a manager and not a top management team then demographic characteristics do have an impact on the decision making and strategic orientation however these characteristics do not directly influence strategic alliance decisions rather there is correlation between strategy and strategic alliances.

- It is possible to say that SME managers can be identified as formal and informal planners and that this may vary depending on the sector and the life cycle of the firm. Managers need to remain proactive throughout their life cycle so that they become proactive managers and not crisis managers. Managers of SMEs need to be committed to innovation to enable them to form relationships and adopt strategic orientation for firm performance.

H_2 There is significant correlation between firms demographics and background characteristics and successful strategic alliances.

9.2.2 Firm demographics (SMEs)

- The empirical findings of this research is confirmatory of existing research that SMEs are not only the back bone of the UK economy but have the ability to remain flexible in their planning while adopting strategic planning techniques as needed.

- The majority of the firms are involved in the development or sophisticated use of technology in their research and development. They are able to attract well-qualified staff that through personal development they are able to retain. The studied firms have a range of products at different stages although the older firms appeared to have found their market and remained focused on a small number of products that they market well, the younger firms were experimenting with research and development and did not generate many sales. For some of the firms long clinical or other trials were required and for this continuous investment was required with immediate access to customers to engage in the trials where appropriate. Innovative strategies enable firms to create a unique and sustainable competitive advantage by creating the products and services for the customers.

- Empirical findings in this study indicate that employers who provide autonomy find employee satisfaction (through retention) and customer goal achievement and that their products through collaboration reach market on time.

- All the firms operate in highly competitive environments and through the use of practices normally associated with larger firms they are able to successfully monitor and analyse their environments to remain competitive. In areas where they are resource strained or lacking in capabilities, they are proactive in sourcing and taking advantage of those available elsewhere.

9.3 Theoretical contributions of the research

The profile of management, SMEs and strategic alliance behaviour have been presented in chapter six to demonstrate a contemporary face of managers today. The interpretations of the findings are presented in chapter eight together with their relation to existing theory. Some of the findings in particular the profiles offer support to existing theory with some modifications as incumbent theory reflects the practice in larger firms this contribution presents a picture of the SME manager and what influences their behaviour providing a benchmark for future management decision making. As presented in chapter three i.e. the literature review there has been little empirical research directly related to demographics and motivation of management in SMEs towards strategic alliances and their success and the original review had to rely on strategic management and alliance literature generally. Therefore, this research may contribute towards the knowledge by explaining the behaviour of managers in SMES in the high tech sector and their ability to manage strategic alliances as a source of strategic growth and the strategy and tools that they employ to do this.

In the first section profiles of the managers were drawn up with some explanation of how these demographics influenced their behaviour. The relationship between a manager's demographics such as age, gender, education etc and their background characteristics such as experience and their perceptions of alliance motivation were identified and discussed. It can be concluded that management demographics do affect their perceptions, however a combination of variables that include environmental, firm and managers need to be considered. As stated previously the research was based on the theory that there would be an effect of one on the other. To clarify management demographics will impact on their use of business tools to carry out environmental scanning this in turn will provide them with data upon which they need to act for example a barrier to markets may result in the manager considering a strategic alliance for marketing purposes. If he had not carried out the scanning then he may have not been aware of the problem until he encountered it, at this stage he would have been reactive to the crisis and as a result experienced failure.

9.4   Policy implications

It is unarguable through the incumbent literature that SMEs make a significant contribution to the UKs economy. SMEs by their entrepreneurial nature are conceded to be a major contributor to innovation and new product creation stimulating competition both domestically and globally. The OECD (2005) report that they are critical to the future economy and will play a significant role as traditional manufacturing gives way to technology development and will therefore remain a focus for policy makers.

This research may be beneficial to policy makers as they are presented with a picture of the SME manager and the motivations for their behaviour. Management practices are disclosed and policy makers may be arbitrators in future alliance development. It is reported that many small business fail each year and the current government have initiatives in place both financially and structurally to assist organic firms. This research will help policy makers understand that production is not the only consideration but that small firms need to be market aware and guidelines and practical support should emphasis this. As this research has highlighted the importance of strategic management to firms of all sizes and the importance of establishing and maintaining relationships resulting in successful alliances then government policy should also reflect this, placing safeguards for young firms from predatory firms.

While this research has found that firms are able to recruit and retain sufficient numbers of scientific staff literature suggests that this is not the case in all situations therefore the policy makers need to ensure future investment in education and training for the SET industries. As well as this specific training it is also noted that explicit managerial training is necessary as many of the managers surveyed are technically competent but do not have all the managerial knowledge to successfully grow their business. For example the government invites innovation but provides little opportunity to match this with market demands.

To conclude there needs to be a pro active move by policy makers to put emphasis on a holistic management training package that synthesise with technology needs. Other government supported agencies may also benefit from this research as many are concerned with the training of managers and providing training in management and business planning.

9.5 Managerial implications

This research has highlighted both the emotional and financial investment owner managers of SMEs make in their businesses. Management demographics significantly impact on managerial behaviour and style of managing and their perceptions on the best methods for the business.

Therefore managers attention to detail and learning from experienced manages can avoid pitfalls of strategic alliances and reap the benefits of successfully brokering and managing them through to completion and achievement of goals.

Managers need to employ management tools to gain an understanding of the industry in which they operate. Carrying out analysis of the environment and employing tools such as SWOT, Porters Five Forces and Pest will enable firms to collect information about the competition and initiate strategies rather than become crisis managers.

The findings show that firms which are managed by committed managers are more likely to be successful in both engaging with partners and managing the alliance.

9.6   Limitations of the study

While the study is intensive it does have two significant limitations and one minor. The main limitation comes from the sample for the study.

The survey was sent to randomly targeted SMEs in the high tech sector and the research may have benefitted from focusing on one sector as undertaken in prior research, however as all firm types under the manufacturing SIC codes were targeted it is feasible that the findings could have been generalised for other sectors both in the high tech sector and those classified under other codes. The findings from the experienced firms could be used as benchmarks for other firms across all sectors.

In obtaining the data through postal survey I have had to rely on the understanding of respondents when interpreting the questions and make the assumption that it is the manager who has completed the survey and not passed it to an employee for completion.

This study may have benefitted from a longitudinal study.

9.7   Suggestions for further research

Given that there have been some limitations to the research and also areas where insufficient data has been collected some areas for future research are discussed below. As there has been a concentration of SMEs in the high tech sector to reduce the limitations of this research a replication of the research across other sectors may reveal results which can reveal a more holistic behaviour pattern of managers of SMEs. Further research might overcome the limited area of strategic management and look at the strategic management process in smaller SMES in the high tech industry.

Further research could be undertaken into who the alliances have been made with and what the contributing factors to their success or failure actually are. Are they the same critical factors as perceived by the managers in this study or are they more complicated? The research could be replicated across different sectors and also looking at firms who operate globally to identify patterns of behaviour which result in the success or failure of strategic alliances as a result of management practice.

Lastly as the unit of analysis for this study was managers of small high tech firms based in the UK an important sector of the economy recognised not only by UK government but also European and indeed worldwide, therefore it would be appropriate to replicate the study in other countries and even to make a comparison of the characteristics of different European SMEs. This would enable further identification of areas where policy makers can help SMEs especially in the competitive global markets.

Further research into the drivers for the firms may also help identify how strategies are devised.

9.8   Chapter summary

This chapter has summarised the implications of the research in terms of managerial, academic and policy maker needs. Limitations of the study have been addressed and the research propositions have been revisited and major findings which were discussed in chapter eight are summarised.

To conclude this research has used prior research to form research questions which have been addressed using empirical research into the management of SMES in the high tech sector in the UK. The research process and the findings have all been discussed with some interpretation of why the results may have occurred.

Bibliography

Adams, R., Bessant, J. and Phelps, R. (2006), Innovation management measurement: A review, International Journal of Management Reviews, Vol. 8, pp. 21–47.

Adcroft, A. and Willis, R. (2008) A snapshot of strategy research 2002-2006. Journal of Management History, Vol. 14 No. 4, pp.. 313-333

Adobor, H. (2006) Optimal trust? Uncertainty as a determinant and limit to trust in inter-firm alliances, Leadership & Organization Development Journal Vol. 27 No. 7 pp. 537-553

Agarwal, R. and Audretsch, D. B. (2001) Does Entry Size Matter? The Impact of the Life Cycle and Technology on Firm Survival, The Journal of Industrial Economics, Vol. 49, No. 1, pp. 21-43

Aggarwal, V. and Hsu, D. (2009) Modes of cooperative R&D commercialization by start-ups, Strategic Management Journal, Vol. 30, pp.. 835-864

Alvesson, M. and Karreman, D. (2001) Odd Couple: Making Sense Of The Curious Concept Of Knowledge Management, Journal of Management Studies, Vol. 38, No. 7, pp. 995-1018

Alvesson, M. and Sveningsson, S. (2003) Good Visions, Bad Micro-management and Ugly Ambiguity: Contradictions of (Non-) Leadership in a

Knowledge-intensive Organization, Organization Studies, Vol. 24, No. 6, pp. 961-988

Analoui, F. and Karami, A. (2003) Strategic Management in small and medium enterprises, Thomson Learning

Andersen, J. (2011) Strategic resources and firm performance, Management Decision, Vol. 49, No. 1, pp.. 87-98

Arikan, A. K. MCgahan, A. (2010) Research notes and commentaries: The development of capabilities in new firms Strategic Management Journal Vol. 31, pp.. 1-18

Avlonitis, G. J. and Salavou, H. E. (2007) Entrepreneurial orientation of SMEs, product innovativeness, and performance, Journal of Business Research, Vol. 60, pp. 566–575

Baloh, P., Jha, S. and Awazu, Y. (2008) Building strategic partnerships for managing innovation outsourcing: Strategic Outsourcing: An International Journal, Vol. 1, No. 2, pp.

Bantel, K. A. (1997) performance in adolescent, technology-based firms:product strategy, implementation, and synergy, The Journal of High Technology Management Research, Vol. 8, No. 2, pp. 243-262

Barnes, D. (2001) Research methods for the empirical investigation of the process of formation of operations strategy, International Journal of Operations &

Barrett, R, and Wynarczyk, P. (2009) Building the science and innovation base: work, skills and employment issues, New Technology, Work and Employment, Vol. 24, No. 3, pp. 210-214

Battisti, G. and Stoneman, P. (2009) How Innovative are UK firms? Evidence from the 4th Community Innovation Survey (CIS4) on the Synergistic Effects of Innovations

Berg M, (1985) The age of manufacturers 1700-1820 Fontana Paperbacks

Berry, M. M. J. (1996) Technical entrepreneurship, strategic awareness and corporate transformation in small high tech firms, Technovation, Vol. 16, No. 9, pp. 487-498

Berry, M. M. J, and Taggart, H. (1998) Combining technology and corporate strategy in small high tech firms, Research Policy, Vol. 26, pp. 883-895

Beverland, M, Bretherton P, (2001) The uncertain search for opportunities: determinants of strategic alliances, Qualitative Market Research An International Journal Vol. 4 No. 2 pp. 88-99

Bizan, O. (2003) The determinants of success of R&D projects: evidence from American–Israeli research alliances, Research Policy Vol. 32, pp. 1619–1640

Bjerregaard, T. (2010) Industry and academia in convergence: Micro-institutional dimensions of R & D Collaboration. Technovation. Vol, 30. pp. 100-108

Bogers, M. (2011) The open innovation paradox:knowledge sharing and protection in R&D collaborations, European Journal of Innovation Management, Vol. 14, No. 1, pp. 93-117

Boyett, I. (1997) The public sector entrepreneur – a definition, International Journal of Entrepreneurial Behaviour & Research, Vol. 3, No. 2, pp. 77-92.

Bregman, A., Fuss, M. and Regev, H. (1991) High tech and productivity Evidence from Israeli industrial firms, European Economic Review, Vol. 35 pp. 1199-1221

Brinckmann, J., Grichnik, D. and Kapsa, D. (2010) Should entrepreneurs plan or just storm the castle? A meta-analysis on contextual factors impacting the business planning–performance relationship in small firms, Journal of Business Venturing, Vol. 25. pp. 24-40

Brown, J. S. and Dugaid, P. (1991) Organizational Learning and Communities-of-Practice: Toward A Unified View of Working, Learning and Innovation, Organization Science, Vol. 2, No. 1, pp. 40-57

Burke, G. and Jarratt, D. (2004) The influence of information and advice on competitive strategy definition in small- and medium-sized enterprises, Qualitative Market Research: An International Journal, Vol. 7, No. 2, pp. 126-138

Busi, M. McIvor, R. (2008) Setting the outsourcing research agenda: the top-10 most urgent outsourcing areas, Strategic Outsourcing: An International Journal Vol. 1, No. 3, pp. 185-197

Byars, L. (1987) Strategic management planning and implementation concepts & cases 2nd Edition

Calof, J. and Wright, S. (2008) Competitive Intelligence: A practitioner, academic and inter-disciplinary perspective, European Journal of Marketing, Vol. 42, No. 7/8, pp. 717-730

Cantner, U., Joel, K. and Schmidt, T. (2009) The use of knowledge management by German innovators, Journal of Knowledge Management, Vol. 13, No. 4, pp. 187-203

Carmen, C., Luz, F. and Salustiano, M. (2006) Influence of top management team vision and work team characteristics on innovation The Spanish case, European Journal of Innovation management, Vol. 9, No. 2, pp. 179-201

Carmichael, J. (1995) What do we believe makes a good manager? Management Development Review, Vol. 8, No. 2, pp. 7-10

Casper, S. and Matraves, C. (2003) Institutional frameworks and innovation in the German and UK pharmaceutical industry, Research Policy, Vol.32, pp. 1865–1879

Cefis, E. and Marsili, O. (2006) Survivor: The role of innovation in firms' survival, Research Policy, Vol. 35, pp. 626–641

Cetindamar, D, and Ulusoy, G, (2008) Innovation performance and partnerships in manufacturing firms in Turkey, Journal of Manufacturing Technology Management, Vol. 19, No. 3, PP. 332-345

Chakravarthy, B. and Lorange, P. (2008) Driving renewal: the entrepreneur-manager, Journal Of Business Strategy, Vol. 29, No. 2, pp. 14-21

Chang, S. and Lee, M. (2008) The linkage between knowledge accumulation capability and organizational innovation, Journal Of Knowledge Management, Vol. 12, No. 1, pp. 3-20

Chao, Y. (2011) Decision making Biases in the Alliance Life Cycle: Implications for Alliance Failure, Management Decision, Vol. 49, No. 3,

Chen, D. and Karami, A. (2010) Critical success factors in inter-firm technological cooperation: an empirical study of high-tech SMEs in China, International Journal of Technology Management, Vol. 51, Nos. 2/3/4/, pp. 282-299

Chen, S., Lee, H. and Wu, Y. (2008) Applying ANP approach to partner selection for strategic alliance, Management Decision, Vol. 46, No. 3, pp. 449-465

Chen, Y. and Wu, T. (2007) An empirical analysis of core competence for high-tech firms and traditional manufacturers, Journal of Management Development, Vol. 26, No. 2, pp. 159-168

Chiaroni, D., Chiesa, V. and Frattini, F. (2009) Investigating the adoption of open innovation in the bio-pharmaceutical industry A framework and an empirical analysis, European Journal of Innovation Management, Vol. 12, No. 3, pp. 285-305

Chiesa, V., Frattini, F., Lazzarotti, V. and Manzini, R. (2009) Performance measurement of research and development activities, European Journal of Innovation Management, Vol. 12, No. 1, pp. 25-61

Chin, K., Chan, B. L. and Lam, P. (2008) Identifying and prioritizing critical success factors for coopetition strategy, Industrial Management & Data Systems, Vol. 108, No. 4, pp. 437-454

Chorev, S. and Anderson, A. R. (2006) Success in Israeli high-tech start-ups; Critical factors and process, Technovation, Vol. 26, pp. 162–174

Chou, C. and Yang, K. (2011) The interaction effect of strategic orientations on new product performance in the high-tech industry: A nonlinear model, Technological Forecasting & Social Change, Vol. 78, pp. 63–74

Clarke-Hill, C., Li, H. and Davies, B. (2003) The paradox of co-operation and competition in strategic alliances: Towards a multi-paradigm approach, Management Research News, Vol. 26, No. 1

Clemens, B. and Bakstran, L (2010) A framework of theoretical lenses and strategic purposes to describe relationships among firm environmental strategy, financial performance, and environmental performance, Management Research Review, Vol. 33, No. 4, pp. 393-405

Coad, A. and Rao, R. (2008) Innovation and firm growth in high-tech sectors:A quantile regression approach, Research Policy, Vol. 37, pp. 633–648

Cooper, A.C. (1973), "Technical entrepreneurship: what do we know?" Research and Developement Management, Vol.3 No. 2, pp. 59-64

Cooper, A. C., Willard, G. E. and Woo, C. Y. (1986) Strategies of high performing new and small firms: A reexamination of the niche concept, Journal of Business Venturing, Vol. 1, pp. 247-260

Cooper, R. G. (1944) Perspective Third-Generation New Product Processes, Journal of Production Innovation Management, Vol. 11, pp.3-14

Cooper, R. G. (1984) New Product Strategies: What Distinguishes the Top Performers?   Journal of Production Innovation Management, Vol. 2, pp.151-164

Cooper, R. G. and Kleinschmidt, E. J. (1986) An Investigation in to the new product process: steps, Deficiencies, and Impact, Journal of Product Innovation Management, Vol. 71, No. 3, pp. 71-85

Cooper, R. G. and Kleinschmidt, E. J. (1993) Major New Products: What Distinguishes the Winners in the Chemical Industry?   Journal of Product Innovation Management, Vol. 10, pp. 90-111

Covin, J. G. And Slevin, D. P. (1998) Adherence to plans, risk taking and environment as predictors of firm growth, The Journal of High Technology Management Research, Vol. 9, No. 2, pp. 207-237

Cravens, D., Piercy, N. and Low, G. (2002) Proactive Cannibalisation and discontinuous technology, European Business Review, Vol. 14, No. 4, pp. 257-267

275

Cui, H. and Mak, Y. T. (2002) The relationship between managerial ownership and firm performance in high R&D firms, Journal of Corporate Finance, Vol. 8, pp. 313–336

Cullen, J. B., Johnson, J. L. and Sakano, S. (2000) Success Through Commitment and Trust: The Soft Side of Strategic Alliance Management, Journal of World Business, Vol. 35, No. 3, pp.223-240

Curran, C., Niedergassel, B., Picker, S. and Leker, J (2009) Project leadership skills in cooperative projects, Management Research News, Vol. 32, No. 5, pp. 458-468

Currie, G. and Kerrin, M. (2003) Human resource management and knowledge management: enhancing knowledge sharing in a pharmaceutical company, The International Journal of Human Resource Management, Vol. 16, No.6, pp. 1027-1045

Dangelico, R., Garavelli, A. and Petruzzelli, A, (2010) A system dynamics model to analyze technology districts' evol.ution in a knowledge-based perspective, Technovation, Vol. 30, pp.142-153

Dankbaar, G., Groenegwgen J. and Schenk H. (eds) perspectives in industrial economics Dordrecht:Kluwer, pp171-95

Das, T. K. and He, I. (2006) Entrepreneurial firms in search of established partners: review and recommendations, International Journal of Entrepreneurial Behaviour & research, Vol. 12, No. 3, pp. 114-143

Das, T. K. and Kumar, R. (2007) Learning dynamics in the alliance development process, Management Decision, Vol. 45, No. 4, pp..684-707

Das, T. K. and Kumar, R. (2010) Interpartner sensemaking in strategic alliances, Management Decision, Vol. 48, No. 1, pp. 17-36

Das, T. K. and Teng, B.S. (2000) A Resource-Based Theory of Strategic Alliances, Journal of Management, Vol. 26, No. 1, pp. 31–61

Day, J., Reynolds, P. and Lancaster, G. (2006) Entrepreneurship and the small to medium-sized enterprise A divergent/convergent paradox in thinking patterns between advisers and SME owner-managers, Management Decision, Vol. 44, No. 5, pp. 581-597

Dealtry, R. (2005) Configuring the structure and administration of learning, Management, Journal of Workplace Learning, Vol. 17, No. 7, pp. 467-477

Dealtry, R. (2008) Exploration of a contextual management framework for strategic learning alliances, Journal of Workplace Learning, Vol. 20, No. 6, pp. 443-452

Dean, A. and Shepherd, D. A. (2010) Multilevel Entrepreneurship Research: Opportunities for Studying Entrepreneurial Decision Making, Journal of Management Online First, published on May 5, 2010 as doi:10.1177/0149206310369940

Deeds, D., DeCarolis, D. and Coombs, J. (1999) Dynamic capabilities and new product Development in High Technology Ventures: An empirical analysis of new Biotechnology Firms, Journal of Business Venturing, Vol. 15, pp. 211-229

Delmar, F., Davidsson, P. and Gartner, W. B. (2003) Arriving at the high-growth firm, Journal of Business Venturing Vol. 18, pp. 189-216

Devlin, G. and Bleackley, M. (1988) Strategic Alliances – Guidelines for Success, Long Range Planning, Vol. 21, No. 5, pp. 18-23

De Wit, B. and Meyer, R. (2010) Strategy Synbook Resolving strategy paradoxes to create competitive advantage, 3rd Edition, United Kingdom Cengage Learning EMEA

Ding, X., Verma, R. and Iqbal, Z. (2007) Self-service technology and online financial service choice, International Journal of Service Industry Management, Vol. 18, No. 3, pp. 246-268

Dobbs, M. and Hamilton, R. (2007) Small business growth: recent evidence and new directions, International Journal of Entrepreneurial Behaviour and Research, Vol. 13, No.5, pp. 296-322

Dodourova, M. (2009) Alliances as strategic tools A cross industry study of partnership planning, formation and success, Management Decision, Vol. 47, No. 5, pp. 831-844

Doganova, L. and Eyquem-Renault, M. (2009) What do business models do? Innovation devices in technology entrepreneurship, Research Policy, Vol. 38, pp. 1559-1570

Dong, L. and Glaister, K. W. (2006) Motives and partner selection criteria in international strategic alliances: Perspectives of Chinese firms, International Business Review, Vol. 15, pp. 577-600

Drago, W. (1997) When strategic alliances make sense, Industrial management & data systems, Vol. 97, No. 2, pp. 53-57

Duysters, G. M., Heimeriks, K. H. and Jurriëns, J. (2003) Three Levels of Alliance Management, Working Paper 03.20, Eindhoven Centre for Innovation Studies, Department of Technology Management

Duysters, G. M., Kok, G. and Vaandrager, M. (1999) Crafting successful strategic technology partnerships, Research and Development Management, Vol. 29, No. 4, pp. 343-351

Dvir, D., Sadeh, A. and Malach-Pines (2010) The fit between entrepreneurs' personalities and the profile of the ventures they manage and business success: An exploratory study, Journal of High Tech Management Research, doi:10.1016/j.hitech.2010.02.006

Dvir, D. and Shenhar, A. (1990) Success Factors Of High-Tech SBUs: Towards a Conceptual Model Based on the Israeli Electronics and Computers Industry, Journal of product innovation management, Vol. 7, pp. 288-296

Eisner, A., Rahman, N. and Korn, H. (2009) Formation conditions, innovation and learning in R&D consortia, Management Decision, Vol. 47, No. 6, pp. 851-871

Elmuti, D., Abebe, M. and Nicolosi, M. (2005) An overview of strategic alliances between universities and corporations, The Journal of Workplace Learning, Vol. 17, No. 1/2, pp. 115-129

Elsbach, K. D., Sutton, R. I. and Whetten, D. A. (1999) Perspectives On Developing Management Theory, Circa 1999: Moving From Shrill Monologues To (Relatively) Tame Dialogues, Academy of Management Review, Vol. 24, No. 4, pp. 627-633.

Engestrom, Y. (2004) New forms of learning in co-configuration work, Journal of Workplace Learning, Vol. 16, No. 1/2, pp. 11-21

Escriba-Esteve, A. and Urra-Urbieta, J. (2002) An analysis of co-operative agreements from a knowledge-based perspective: an integrative conceptual framework, Journal of Knowledge Management, Vol. 6, No. 4, pp. 330-346

Espino-Rodriguez, T. F. and Rodriguez, D. M, (2008) Effects of internal and relational capabilities on outsourcing: an integrated model, Industrial, Management & Data Systems, Vol. 108, No. 3, pp. 328-345

Felsenstein, D. (1994) University-related Science parks – 'seedbeds' or 'enclacves' of innovation? Technovation, Vol. 14, No. 2, pp. 93-110

Fening, F., Pesakivic, G. and Amaria, P. (2008) Relationship between quality management practices and the performance of small and medium size enterprises (SMEs) in Ghana, International Journal of Quality & Reliability Management, Vol. 25, No. 7, pp. 694-708

Fiat, J. (2008) Prescriptive Entrepreneurship Edward Elgar Publishing Limited

Floren, H. (2003) Collaborative approaches to management learning in small firms, Journal of workplace learning, Vol. 15, No. 5, pp.203-216

Ford, D., Gadde, L., Hakansson, H. and Snehota, I. (2003) Managing Business Relationships 2nd Edition, John Wiley & Sons

Freeman, S., Hutchings, K., Lazaris, M. and Zyngier, S. (2010) A model of rapid knowledge development: The smaller born-global firm, International Business Review Vol. 19, pp. 70-84

French, S. (2009a) Cogito ergo sum: exploring epistemological options for strategic management, Journal of Management Development, Vol. 28, No. 1, pp. 18-37

French, S. (2009b) Critiquing the language of strategic management, Journal of Management Development, Vol. 28, No.1, pp. 6-17

French, S. (2004) The role of strategic planning in the performance of small professional service firms, Journal of Management Development, Vol.23, No.8, pp. 765-776

Garbuio, M., Wilcox King, A. and Dan Lovallo, D. (2011) Looking Inside: Psychological Influences on Structuring a Firm's Portfolio of Resources, Journal of Management published online 6 January 2011

Garcia-Valderrama, T., Mulero-Mendigorri, M. and Revuelta-Bordoy, D. (2008) A Balanced Scorecard framework for R&D, European Journal of Innovation Management, Vol. 11, No. 2, pp. 241-281

Ghosh, A. (2004) Learning in strategic alliances A Vygotskian perspective. The Learning Organisation, Vol. 11, No. 4/5, pp. 302-311

Glaister K, et al, (2008) A causal analysis of formal strategic planning and firm performance Evidence from an emerging country Management Decision Vol.46 No.3 pp. 365-391

Goll, I., Johnson, N. and Rasheed, A. (2008) Top Management team demographic characteristics, business strategy, and firm performance in the US airline industry, Management Decision, Vol. 46, No. 2, pp. 201-222

Goold, M. and Cambell, A. (1987) many best ways to make strategy Harvard Business Review nov-dec

Gower, S. Harris, F. (1996) Evaluating British science parks as property investment opportunities, Journal of property Valuation & Investment, Vol. 14, No. 2, pp. 24-37

Grabher, G., (1993) The embedded firm On the socioeconomics of industrial networks Routledge

Grant, R. M and Baden-Fuller, C. (2004) A Knowledge Accessing Theory of Strategic Alliances, Journal of Management Studies, Vol. 41, No. 1, pp. 61-84

Gravier, M. J., Wesley S. Randall, W. S. and Strutton, D. (2008) Investigating the role of knowledge in alliance performance, Journal Of Knowledge Management, Vol. 12, No. 4, pp. 117-130

Green, R., David, J., Dent, M. and Tyshkovsky, A. (1996) The Russian entrepreneur: a study of psychological characteristics, International Journal of Entrepreneurial Behaviour & Research, Vol. 2, No. 1, pp. 49-58.

Greiner, L. (1972) Evolution and Revolution as Organisations Grow: A company's past has clues for management that are critical to future success, Family Business Review, Vol. 10, No. 4, pp.397-409

Grinstein, A. and Goldman, A. (2006) Characterizing the technology firm: An exploratory study, Research Policy, Vol. 35, pp. 121-143

Gujarati, D. (2003) Basic Econometrics 4th Edition McGraw Hill

Gulati, R., Lavie, D. and Singh, H. (2009) The nature of partnering experience and the gains from alliances Strategic Management Journal, Vol. 30, pp. 1213-1233

Gummesson, E. (1994) Making Relationship Marketing Operational, International Journal of Service Industry Management, Vol. 5, No. 5, pp. 5-20.

Haesli, A. and Boxall, P. (2005) 'When knowledge management meets HR strategy: an exploration of personalization-retention and codification-recruitment configurations', The International Journal of Human Resource Management, Vol. 16, No. 11, pp. 1955-1975

Haeusssler, C., Patzelt, H. and Zahra, S. (2010) Strategic alliances and product development in high technology new firms: The moderating effect of technological capabilities, Journal of Business Venturing

Hagedoorn, J. (1990) Organisational modes of interfirm cooperation and technology transfer, Technovation, Vol. 10, No. 1, pp. 17-30

Hagedoorn, J. (1996) Trends and Patterns in Strategic Technology Partnering Since the early Seventies, Review of industrial organisation, Vol. 11, pp. 601-616

Hagedoorn, J. (2002) Inter-firm R&D partnerships: an overview of major trends and patterns since 1960, Research Policy, Vol. 31, pp. 477-492

Hagedoorn, J. and Schakenraad, J. (1994) The effect of strategic technology alliances on company performance, Strategic Management Journal, Vol. 15, pp. 291-309

Hagedoorn, J. and Duysters, G. (2002) External sources of Innovative Capabilities: The Preference for Strategic Alliances or Mergers and Acquisitions, Journal of Management Studies, Vol. 39, No. 2, pp 167-188

Hamilton, R. T. and Harper, D. A. (1994) The Entrepreneur in Theory and Practice, Journal of Economic Studies, Vol. 2, No. 6, pp. 3-18

Harrison, J. S. (2003) Strategic Management of resources and relationships, New York, John Wiley & Sons

Harrison, J. and Taylor, B. (1996) Supergrowth Companies Entrepreneurs in Action Butterworth Heinemann

Hart, S. J. and Baker, M. J. (1994) The Multiple Convergent Processing Model of New Product Development, International Marketing Review, Vol. 11, No. 1, pp. 77-92

Hassanain, M. and Al-Saadi, S. (2005) A framework model for outsourcing asset management, Services Facilities, Vol. 23, No. 1/2, pp. 73-81

Herbane, B. (2010) Small business research: Time for a crisis-based view, International Small Business Journal, Vol. 28, No. 1, pp. 43-64

Himmelberg, C. P. and Petersen, B. C. (1994) R & D and Internal Finance: A Panel Study of Small Firms in High-Tech Industries, The Review of Economics and Statistics, Vol. 76, No. 1, pp. 38-51

Hislop, D. (2001) Mission impossible? Communicating and sharing knowledge via information technology, Journal of information Technology, Vol. 17, pp.165-177

Hitt, M., Ireland, R., Camp, S. and Sexton, D. (2001) Strategic Entrepreneurship: Entrepreneurial Strategies for Wealth Creation, Strategic Management Journal, Vol. 22, pp. 479-491

Hoffman, K. et al, (1998) Small Firms, R&D, technology and innovation in the UK:a literature review, Technovation, Vol.18, No. 1, pp. 39-55

Hoffmann, W. H. and Schlosser, R. (2001) Success Factors of Strategic Alliances in Small and Medium-sized Enterprises—An Empirical survey, Long Range Planning, Vol. 34, pp. 357-381

Holtzman, Y. (2008) Innovation in research and development: tool of strategic growth, Journal of Management Development, Vol. 27, No. 10, pp. 1037-1052

Horton, V. (1998) An exploration of strategic collaboration in the Triad, European Business Review, Vol. 98, No. 1, pp. 4-12

Horwitz, F. M., Heng, C. T. and Quazi, H. A. (2003) Finders, keepers? Attracting, motivating and retaining knowledge workers, Human Resource Management Journal, Vol. 13, No. 4, pp. 23-44

Hotho, S. and Champion, K. (2011) Small businesses in the new creative industries: innovation as a people management challenge, Management Decision, Vol. 49, No. 1, pp. 29-54

Hough, J. R. and White, M. A. (2004) Scanning actions and environmental dynamism Gathering information for strategic decision Making, Management Decision, Vol. 42, No. 6, pp. 781-793

Hughes, S. and Beasley, F. (2008) A Framework for Strategic Alliance Partner Choice, Journal of Business Inquiry, pp. 53-60

Jack, E. and Raturi, A. (2006) Lessons learned from methodical triangulation in management research, Management Research News, Vol. 29, No. 6, pp. 346-357

Jackson, S. (2007) Market share is not enough: why strategic market positioning works, Journal of Business Strategy, Vol. 28, No. 1, pp. 18-25

Jamali, D. (2005) Changing management paradigms: implications for educational institutions, Journal of Management Development, Vol. 24, No. 2, pp. 104-115

Jarratt, D. (1998) A strategic classification of business alliances: a qualitative perspective built from a study of small and medium-sized enterprises, Qualitative market research: An international journal, Vol. 1, No. 1, pp. 39-49

Jarratt, D. (2008) Testing a theoretically constructed relationship management capability, European Journal of Marketing, Vol. 42, No. 9/10, pp. 1106-1132

Jauch, L. and Glueck, W. (1988) Business Policy and strategic management 5th Edition Mcgraw Hill

Jiang, X., Li, Y. and Gao, S. (2008) The stability of strategic alliances: Characteristics, factors and stages, Journal of International Management, Vol. 14, pp. 173-189

Jocumsen, G. (2004) How do small business managers make strategic marketing decisions? European Journal of Marketing, Vol. 38, No. 5/6, pp. 659-674

Johnson, G., Scholes, K. and Whittington, R. (2008) Exploring Corporate Strategy Text & Cases 8th Edition Prentice Hall

Johnston, M., Gilmore, A. and Carson, D. (2008) Dealing with environmental Uncertainty The value of scenario planning for small to medium-sized enterprises (SMEs), European Journal of Marketing, Vol. 42, No. 11/12, pp. 1170-1178

Joia, L. and Malheiros, R. (2009) Strategic alliances and the intellectual capital of firms, Journal of Intellectual Capital, Vol. 10, No. 4, pp. 539-558

Jones, E., Chonko, L. and Roberts, J. (2003) Creating a partnership-orientated knowledge creation culture in strategic sales alliances: a conceptual framework, Journal of Business & Industrial Marketing, Vol. 18, No. 4/5, pp. 336-352

Jones-Evans, D, and Westhead, P, (1996) "The high technology small firm sector in the UK" International Journal of Entrepreneurial Behaviour & Research, Vol. 2, No. 1, pp. 15-35

Jones, R. and Rowley, J. (2011) Networks and Customer Relationships in a Small Software Technology Firm: A Case Study, Journal of Small Business and Entrepreneurship Vol. 24, 1, pp. 29-48

Ju, T., Chen, S., Chia-Ying, L. and Tien Shiang, L, (2005) A strategic contingency model for technology alliance, Industrial Management & Data Systems ,Vol. 105, No. 5, pp. 623-644

Kakati, M. (2003) Success criteria in high-tech new ventures, Technovation, Vol. 23, pp. 447-457

Kala, S., Retna, K. S. and Ng, P. K. (2011) Communities of practice: dynamics and success factors, Leadership & Organization, Development Journal, Vol. 32, No. 1, pp. 41-59

Karami, A. (2007) Strategy Formulation in Entrepreneurial Firms Ashgate

Karami, A., Analoui, F. and Kakabadse, N. (2006) The CEOs' characteristics and their strategy development in the UK SME sector An empirical study, Journal of Management Development, Vol. 25, No. 4, pp. 316-324

Karaev, A., Koh, S. C. and Szamosi, L. T. (2007) The cluster approach and SME competitiveness: a review, Journal of Manufacturing Technology Management, Vol. 18, No. 7, pp. 818-835

Karakaya, F and Kobu, B. (1994) New product Development process: An investigation Of Success and failure in high-Technology and non high-Technology firms, Journal of Business Venturing, Vol. 9, pp. 49-66

Kauer, D., Waldeck, T. and Schaffer, U. (2007) Effects of top management team characteristics on strategic decision making, Management Decision, Vol. 45, No. 6, pp. 334-344 pp. 942-967

Kaynak, H. and Hartley, J. L. (2005) Exploring quality management practices and high tech firm performance, Journal of High Technology Management Research, Vol. 16, pp. 255–272

Keeley, R. H. and Tabrizi, B. (1995) High tech entrepreneurs: Serious competitors or troublemakers? The Journal of High Technology Management Research, Vol. 6, No. 1, pp. 127-143

Kegtibeb, T. (200) Collaborative relationships in facility services, Leadership & Organization Development Journal, Vol. 27, No. 6, pp. 449-464

Kemal, A. R. (1993) Why do small firms fail to graduate to medium and large firms in Pakistan? The Pakistan Development Review, Vol. 32, No. 4, pp.1249-1257

Kezar, A. and Eckel, P. D. (2002) Principles or Culturally Responsive Concepts? The Journal of Higher Education, Vol. 73, No. 4, pp. 435-460

Kodama, K. (2005) Case study How two Japanese high-tech companies achieved rapid innovation via strategic community networks, Strategy & Leadership, Vol. 33, No.6, pp. 39-47

Kohn, K. (2005) Idea generation in new product development through business environmental scanning: the case of XCar, Marketing Intelligence & Planning, Vol. 23, No. 7, pp. 688-704

Kovacic, A. (2007) Benchmarking the Slovenian competitiveness by system of indicators, Benchmarking: An International Journal, Vol. 14, No. 5, pp. 553-574

Kraus, S., Harms, R. and Schwarz, E. (2006) Strategic planning in smaller enterprises-new empirical finding, Management Research News, Vol. 2, No.6

Kumaramangalam, K. (2005) Does collaborating with academia improve industry science? Evidence from the UK biotechnology sector,1988-2001 Aslib Proceedings: New Information Perspectives, Vol. 57, No. 3, pp. 261-277

Laforet, S. (2008) Size, strategic, and market orientation affects on innovation, Journal of Business Research, Vol. 61, pp. 753-764

Laforet, S. (2009) Effects of Size, market and strategic orientation on innovation in non-high-tech manufacturing SMEs, European Journal of Marketing, Vol. 43, No. 1/2, pp. 188-212

Lai, J., Chang, S. and Chen, S. (2010) Is experience valuable in international strategic alliances? Journal of International Management, Vol. 16, pp. 247–261

Lasch, F., Roy, F. and Yami, S. (2007) Critical growth factors of ICT start ups, Management Decision, Vol. 45, No. 1, pp. 62-75

Lau, C., Yiu, D., Yeung, P. and Lu, Y, (2008) Strategic orientation of high-technology firms in a transitional economy, Journal of Business Research, Vol. 61, pp. 765-777

Lawrence, P. and ul-Haq, R. (1998) Qualitative research into strategic alliances, Qualitative market research: An international journal, Vol. 1, No. 1, pp.15-24

Leach, M. (2009) Examining exchange relationships among high-tech firms in the evolving global economy, Journal of Business & Industrial Marketing, Vol. 24 No. 2, pp. 78-85

Lee, C. (2007) Strategic alliances influence on small and medium firm performance, Journal of Business Research, Vol. 60, pp. 731-741

Lee, J., Park, S. H., Ryu, Y. and Baik, Y. (2010) A hidden cost of strategic alliances under Schumpeterian dynamics, Research Policy, Vol. 39, pp. 229–238

Lehtonen, T. (2006) Collaborative relationships in facility services, Leadership & Organization Development Journal, Vol. 27, No. 6, pp. 449-464

Leiponen, A. and Byma, J. (2009) If you cannot block, you better run: Small firms, cooperative innovation, and appropriation strategies, Research Policy, Vol. 38, pp. 1478-1488

Leisen, B., Lilly, B, and Winsor, R. (2002) The effects of organizational, culture and market orientation on the effectiveness of strategic marketing alliances, Journal of Services Marketing, Vol. 16, No. 3, pp. 201-222

Leonard, D.and McAdam, R. (2002) The role of the business excellence model in operational and strategic decision making, Management Decision, Vol. 40, No. 1, pp. 17-25

Leshem, S. and Trafford, V. (2007) Overlooking the conceptual framework, Innovation in Education and Teaching International, Vol. 44, No. 1, pp. 93-105

Li, J., Brake, G., Champion, A., Fuller T., Gabel, S. and Hatcher-Busch (2009) Workplace learning: the roles of knowledge accessibility and management, Journal of Workplace Learning, Vol. 21, No. 4, pp. 347-364

Liao, J. and, Welsch, H. (2008) Patterns of venture gestation process: Exploring the differences between tech and non-tech nascent entrepreneurs, Journal of High Technology Management Research, Vol. 19, pp. 103-113

Lin, B. and Darling, J. (1999) An analysis of the formulation of strategic alliances: a focus on the pharmaceutical industry, Industrial Management & Data Systems, Vol. 99, No. 3, pp. 121-127

Lin, C. and Lin, H. (2010) Maker-buyer strategic alliances: an integrated framework, Journal of Business & Industrial Marketing, Vol. 25, No. 1, pp. 43-56

Lin, C. Y. and Chen, M. Y. (2007) Does innovation lead to performance? An empirical study of SMEs in Taiwan, Management Research News, Vol. 30, No. 2, pp. 115-132

Lin, Z., Yang, H. and Arya, B. (2009) Alliance partners and firm performance resource complementarity and status association, Strategic management journal, Vol. 30 , pp. 921-940

Lindelof, P and Lofsten, H. (2002) Growth, management and financing of new technology-based firms -assessing value-added contributions of firms located on and off Science Parks, The international Journal of management science, Vol. 30, pp. 143-154

Lorange, P. and Roos, J. (1991a) Analytical Steps in the Formation of Strategic Alliances, Journal of Organizational Change Management, Vol. 4, No. 1, pp. 60 – 72

Lorange, P. and Roos, J. (1991b) Why Some Strategic Alliances Succeed and Others Fail, Journal of Business Strategy, Vol. 12, No. 1, pp. 25 - 30

Lorange, P. and Roos, J. (1993) Strategic Alliances Formation, Implementation and Evolution, Blackwell Publishers

Lunnan, R. and Haugland, S. (2008) Research notes and commentaries Predicting and measuring alliance performance: a multidimensional analysis, Strategic Management Journal, Vol. 29, pp. 545-556

Makadok, R. (2010) The Four Theories of Profit and Their Joint Effects, Journal of Management published online 19 October 2010

Mandal, P., Love, P. and Irani Z. (2003) Pre-alliance planning: development of an information system infrastructure to support strategic alliance activities, Management Decision, Vol. 41, No. 2, pp. 132-140

March, I. Gunasekaran, A. (1999) Business strategy in new high tech ventures: an empirical analysis, Management Decision, Vol. 37, No. 3, pp. . 222-232

Mariani, M. (2004) What determines technological hits? Geography versus firm competencies, Research Policy, vol. 33, pp. 1565-1582

Maritan, C. A. and Peteraf, M. A. (2010) Building a Bridge Between Resource Acquisition and Resource Accumulation, Journal of Management, published online 18 November 2010

Marshall, N. (2008) Cognitive and Practice-based Theories of Organisational Knowledge and Learning: Incompatible or Complementary? Management Learning, Vol. 39, No. 4, pp.413-435

Marshall, N. and Brady, T. (2001) Knowledge management and the politics of knowledge: illustrations from complex products and sy

Mason, R. (2007) The external environment's effect on management and strategy A complexity theory approach, Management Decision, Vol. 45, No. 1, pp. 10-28

Mason, R., Lalwani, C. and Boughton, R. (2007) Combining vertical and horizontal collaboration for transport optimisation, Supply Chain Management: An International Journal, Vol. 12, No. 3, pp. 187-199

Massey, G. R. and Dawes, P. L. (2007) Personal characteristics, trust, conflict, and effectiveness in marketing/sales working Relationships, European Journal of Marketing, Vol. 41, No. 9/10, pp. 1117-1145

Maurer, S. D. and Zugelder, M. T. (2000) Trade Secret Management In High Technology: A Legal Review And Research Agenda, The Journal of High Technology Management Research, Vol. 11, No. 2, pp. 155-174

Meade, L. and Sarkis, J. (2002) A conceptual model for selecting and evaluating third-party reverse logistics providers, Supply Chain Management: An International Journal Vol. 7, No. 7, pp. 283-295

Mellat-Parast, Digman L, (2007) A framework for quality management practices in strategic alliances, Management Decision Vol. 45, No. 4, pp. 802-818

McAdam, M. and McAdam, R. (2008) High tech start-ups in University Science Park incubators: The relationship between the start-up's lifecycle progression and use of the incubator's resources, Technovation, Vol. 28, pp. 277–290

McCutchen, W. W. Jr. and Swamidass, P. M. (2004) Motivations for strategic alliances in the pharmaceutical/biotech industry: Some new findings, Journal of High Technology Management Research, Vol. 15, pp. 197-214

McIvor, R, (2000) A practical framework for understanding the outsourcing process, Supply Chain Management: An International Journal, Vol. 5, No. 1, pp. 22-36

Minshall, T., Mortara, L., Elia, S. and Probert, D. (2008) Development of practitioner guidelines for partnerships between start-ups and large firms, Journal of Manufacturing Technology Management, Vol. 19, No. 3, pp. 391-406

Mintzberg, H. (1991) The effective organisation, Sloan Management Review, Vol. Winter, pp. 54-67

Mintzberg, H. (1973) Strategy –making in three modes, California Management Review, Vol. 16, No. 2, pp. 44-53

Miotti, L. and Sachwald, F. (2003) Co-operative R&D: why and with whom? An integrated framework of analysis, Research Policy, Vol. 32, pp. 1481–1499

Mitsuhashi, H. (2002) Uncertainty In Selecting Alliance Partners: The Three Reduction Mechanisms And Alliance Formation Processes, International Journal of Organizational Analysis, Vol. 10, No. 2, pp. 109-133

Morbey, G. K. (1988) R & D: Its relationship to company performance, Journal of Production innovation management, Vol. 3, pp. 191-200

Moriarty, J. and Jones, R. (2008) Marketing in small hotels: a qualitative study, Marketing Intelligence & Planning, Vol. 26, No. 3, pp. 293-315

Mothe, C. and. Quelin, B. V. (2001) Resource creation and partnership in R&D consortia, Journal of High Technology Management Research, Vol. 12, pp.113-138

Murphy, P. J. (2009) Entrepreneurship theory and the poverty of historicism, Journal of Management History, Vol. 15, No. 2, pp. 109-133

Murray, E. A. Jr and. Mahon, J. F. (1993) Strategic Alliances: Gateway to the New Europe? Long Range Planning, Vol. 26, No. 4, pp. 102-111

Naranjo-Valencia, J., Jimenez-Jimenez, D. and Sanz-Valle, R. (2011) Innovation or imitation? The role of organisational culture, Management Decision, Vol. 49, No. 1, pp. 55-72

Narteh, B. (2008) Knowledge transfer in developed-developing country interfirm collaborations: a conceptual framework, Journal of Knowledge Management, Vol. 12, No. 1, pp. 78-91

Neelankavil, J. P. and Alaganar, V. T. (2003) Strategic resource commitment of high-technology firms An international comparison, Journal of Business Research, Vol. 56, pp. 493–502

Neilson, R. (1997) Collaborative Technologies & Organizational Learning, Idea Group Publishing

Nieto, M. (2004) Basic propositions for the study of the technological innovation process in the firm, European Journal of Innovation Management, Vol. 7, No. 4, pp. 314-324

Norburn, D. and Birley, S. (1988) "The top management team and corporate performance" Strategic Management Journal, Vol. 9, pp. 225-37

O'Regan, N. and Ghobadian, A. (2002) Effective strategic planning in small and medium sized firms, Management Decision, Vol. 40, No. 7, pp. 663-671

O'Regan, N. and Ghobadian, A. (2004) Testing the homogeneity of SMEs The impact of size on managerial and organisational processes, European Business Review, Vol. 16, No. 1, pp. 64-79

O'Regan, N. and Sims, M. A. (2008) Identifying high technology small firms: A sectoral analysis, Technovation, Vol. 28, pp. 408-423

O'Regan, N., Sims, M. A. and Gallear, D. (2008) Leaders, Loungers, Laggards, Journal of Manufacturing Technology, Vol. 19, No.1, pp. 6-21

O'Reilly, P. and Finnegan, P. (2007) B2B marketplaces sharing IS/IT infrastructures: an exploration of strategic technology alliances, Journal of Enterprise Information Management, Vol. 20, No. 3, pp. 304-318

Oxley, J. and Sampson, R. (2004) The scope and governance of international R&D alliances, Strategic Management Journa, Vol. 25, pp. 723-749

Paiva, E. L., Roth, A. V. and Fensterseifer, J. E. (2008) Organizational knowledge and the manufacturing strategy process: A resource-based view analysis, Journal of Operations Management, Vol. 2, pp. 115–132

Pandian, J. and McKiernan, P. (2004) Competence-Based Management And Strategic Alliances, Advances in Applied Business Strategy, Vol. 8, pp. 135-146

Pansiri, J. (2005) The influence of managers' characteristics and perceptions in strategic alliance practice. Management Decision. Vol. 43. No. 9. pp. 1097-1113

Pansiri, J. (2008) The effects of characteristics of partners on strategic alliance performance in the SME dominated travel sector, Tourism Management, Vol, 29, pp. 101-115

Park, S. Kim, D. (1997) Market valuation of joint gains, Journal of Business Venturing, Vol. 12, No. 2, pp.83-108

Parker, H. (2000) Interfirm collaboration and the new product development process, Industrial Management & Data Systems, Vol. 100, No. 6, pp. 255-260

Pasanen, M. and Laukkanen, T. (2006) Team Managed growing SMEs a distinct species? Management Research News, Vol. 29, No.11, pp. 684-700

Pateli, A. G. (2009) Decision making on governance of strategic technology alliances, Management Decision, Vol. 47, No. 2, pp. 246-270

Pedler, M. et al (1991) A strategy for sustainable development 2nd Edition The Learning Company

Pegels, C. and Yang, B. (2000) The impact of managerial characteristics on strategic assets management capabilities, Team Performance Management: An international Journal, Vol. 6, No. 5/6, pp. 97-106

Penrose, E. (1980) The theory of the growth of the firm 2nd Edition Basil Blackwell Publisher

Persona, A., Regattieri, A. and Romano, P. (2004) An integrated reference model for production planning and control in SMEs, Journal of Manufacturing Technology Management, Vol. 15, No. 7, pp. 626-640

Petruzzelli, A., Albino, V. and Carbonara, N. (2007) Technology districts: proximity and knowledge access, Journal of knowledge management, Vol. 11, No. 5, pp. 98-114

Philbin, S. (2008) Process model for university-industry research collaboration, European Journal of Innovation Management, Vol. 11, No. 4, pp. 488-521

Pidduck, A. (2006) Issues in supplier partner selection, Journal of Enterprise Information Management, Vol. 19, No. 3, pp. 262-276

Pollard, D. and Hotho, S. (2006) Crises, scenarios and the strategic management process, Management Decision, Vol. 44, No. 6, pp. 721-736

Porrini, P. (2004) Alliance experience and value creation in high-tech and low-tech acquisitions, Journal of High Technology Management Research, Vol. 15, pp. 267–292

Porter, M. (1996) What is strategy? Harvard Business Review Nov/Dec

Quintas, P., Wield, D. and Massey, D. (1992) Academic-industry links and innovation: questioning the science park model, Technovation, Vol. 12, No. 3, pp. 161-175

Ramaseshan, B. and Loo, P. (1998) Factors affecting a partner's perceived effectiveness of strategic business alliance: some Singaporean evidence, International Business Review, Vol. 7, pp. 443-458

Ramirez, M. and Li, X. (2009) Learning and sharing in a Chinese high-technology cluster: a study of inter-firm and intra-firm knowledge flows between R&D employees New Technology, Work and Employment Vol. 24, No. 3, pp. 277-296

Rhyne, L., Teagarden, M., Lamb, B., Amir, D., Powell, S., Stevens, S. and Wu, J. (1997) Technology based competitive strategy: An empirical Test of an Integrative Model, The Journal of High Technology Management Research, Vol. 8, No. 2, pp. 187-212

Richard, P., Devinney, T., Yip, G. and Johnson, G. (2009) Measuring Organisational Performance: Towards Methodological Best Practice, Journal of Management, Vol. 35, No. 3, pp. 718-804

Robert, F., Marque, P., Lasch, F. and Le Roy, F. (2009) Entrepreneurship in emerging high-tech industries: ICT entrepreneurs between experts and kamikazes, International Journal of Entrepreneurship and Small Business, Vol. 7, No. 3, pp. 258-283

Rogers, E. W. (2001) A theoretical look at firm performance in high-tech organisations What does existing theory tell us? The Journal of High Technology Management Research, Vol. 12, pp. 39-61

Rothaermel, F. T.and Boeker W, (2008) Old Technology meets new technology: Complementarities, Similarities, and alliance formation, Strategic Management Journal, Vol. 29, pp. 47-77

Rothaermel, F. T. and Deeds, D. L. (2006) Alliance type, alliance experience and alliance management capability in high-technology ventures, Journal of Business Venturing, Vol. 21, pp. 429-460

Saffu, K. and Mamman, A. (1999) Mechanics, problems and contributions of tertiary strategic alliances: the case of 22 Australian universities, The international Journal of Educational Management, Vol. 13, No. 6, pp. 281-286

Sanyal, R. and Guvenli, T. (2004) Perception of Managerial characteristics and Organisational Performance: Comparative Evidence from Israel, Slovenia, and

Sarkis, J., Talluri, S. and Gunasekaran, A. (2007) A strategic model for agile virtual enterprise partner selection, International Journal of Operations & Production Management, Vol. 27, No. 11, pp. 1213-1234

Saunders, M, Lewis, and Thornhill (2007) Research Methods for Business Students 4th Edition Prentice Hall

Saxena, K. and Bharadwaj, S. (2009) Managing business processes through outsourcing: a strategic partnering perspective, Business Process Management Journal, Vol. 15, No. 5, pp. 687-715

Schreiner, M., Kale, P. and Corsten, D. (2009) What really is alliance management capability and how does it impact alliance outcomes and success? Strategic Management Journal, Vol. 30, pp. 1395-1419

Segal, G., Borgia, D. and Schoenfeld, J. (2005) The motivation to become an entrepreneur, International Journal of Entrepreneurial Behaviour & Research, Vol. 11, No. 1, pp. 42-57

Selwyn, N. (2002)'E-stablishing' an Inclusive Society? Technology, Social Exclusion and UK Government Policy Making, Journal Social. Policy, Vol. 31, No. 1, pp.1-20

Seymour, D., Crook, D. and Rooke, J. (1997) 'The Role of Theory in Construction Management: A Call for Debate,' Construction Management and Economics, Vol. 15, No. 1, pp. 117-119.

Shah, R. and Swaminathan, V. (2008) Factors influencing partner selection in strategic alliances: The moderating role of alliance context, Strategic Management Journal, Vol. 29, pp. 471-494

Shefer, D. and Frenkel, A. (2005) R&D, Firm size and innovation: an empirical analysis, Technovation, Vol. 25, pp. 25-32

Singh, R. K. and Garg, S. K. (2008) Strategy development by SMEs for competitiveness Benchmarking, An International Journal, Vol. 20, No. 8/9, pp. 525-547

Singh, R. K., Garg, S. K. and Deshmukh, S. G. (2010) Strategy development by small scale industries in India, Industrial Management & Data Systems, Vol. 110, No. 7, pp. 1073-1093

Sirmon, D. G., Hitt, M. A., Ireland, R. D. and Gilbert, B. A. (2010) Resource Orchestration to Create Competitive Advantage: Breadth, Depth, and Life Cycle Effects, Journal of Management published online 1 November 2010

Smallbone, D., Leigh, R. and North, D. (1995) The characteristics and strategies of high growth SMEs, International Journal of Entrepreneurial Behaviour & Research, Vol. 1, No. 3, pp. 44-62

Smart, P., Bessant, J. and Gupta, A. (2007) Towards technological rules for designing innovation networks: a dynamic capabilities view, International Journal of Operations & Production Management, Vol. 27, No. 10, pp. 1069-1092

Smith, D. (2003) Strategic alliances and competitive strategies in the European aerospace industry: the case of BMW Rolls-Royce GmbH, European Business Review, Vol. 15, No. 4, pp. 262-276

Smith, M. A. and Zahrly, J. (1993) Resource Allocation In High Technology Firms: Managerial Strategies And Empirical Results, The Journal of High Technology Management Research, Vol. 4, No. 1, pp. 47-61.

Soosay, C., Hyland, P. and Ferrer, M. (2008) Supply chain collaboration: capabilities for continuous innovation, Supply Chain Management: An International Journal, Vol. 13, No. 2, pp. 160-169

Srinivasan, R., Lilien, G. L. and Rangaswamy A. (2008) Survival of high tech firms: The effects of diversity of product–market portfolios, patents, and trademarks, International. Journal of Research in Marketing, Vol. 25, pp. 119-128

Srivastava, P. and Frankwich, G. (2011) Environment, management attitude, and organisational learning in alliances, Management Decision, Vol. 49, No. 1,

Stewart, W. H., Carland, J. C., Carland J. W., Watson, W. E. and Sweo, R. (2003) Entrepreneurial Dispositions and Goal Orientations: A Comparative Exploration of United States and Russian Entrepreneurs, Journal of Small Business Management, Vol. 4, No.1, pp. 27–46

Stonehouse, G. and Pemberton, J. (2002) Strategic Planning in SMEs some empirical findings, Management Decision. Vol. 40, No. 9, pp. 853-

Stuart, F. I. (1997) Supplier alliance success and failure: a longitudinal dyadic perspective, International Journal of Operations & Production Management, Vol. 17, No. 6, pp. 539-557

Taylor, A. (2005) An operations perspective on strategic alliance success factors An exploratory study of alliance managers in the software industry, International Journal of Operations & Production Management, Vol. 25 No. 5, pp. 469-490,

Teece, D. (1986) Profiting from technological innovation: Implications for integration, collaboration, licensing and public policy Research Policy, Vol. 15, pp. 285-305

Teng, B. and Das, T. K. (2008) Governance structure choice in strategic alliances, The roles of alliance objectives, alliance management experience, and international partners, Management Decision, Vol. 46, No. 5, pp. 725-742

Tetteh, E. and Burn, J. (2001) Global strategies for SMe-business: applying the SMALL framework, Logistics Information Management, Vol. 14, No. 1/2, pp. 171-180

Thomas, P., Moliterno, T. P. and Mahony, D. M. (2010) Network Theory of Organization: A Multilevel Approach, Journal of Management published online 21 July 2010

Thompson, A., Strickland, A. and Fulmer, W. (1984) Readings in strategic Management Business Publications Inc.

Thompson, J. L. (1999) The world of the entrepreneur - a new perspective, Journal of Workplace Learning: Employee Counselling Today, Vol. 11, No. 6, pp. 209-224

Thompson, J. L. (2004) The facets of the entrepreneur: Identifying entrepreneurial potential, Management Decision, Vol. 42, No. 2, pp. 243-258

Todeva, E. and Knoke, D. (2005) Strategic Alliances and models of collaboration, Management Decision, Vol. 43, No. 1, pp. 123-148

Tovstiga, G. and Tulugrova, (2007) Intellectual capital practices and Performance in Russian enterprises, Journal of Intellectual Capital, Vol. 8, No. 4, pp. 695-707

Tsai, K. and Wang, J. (2005) Does R&D performance decline with firm size?—A re-examination in terms of elasticity, Research Policy, Vol. 34, pp. 966-976

Tyler, B. (2001) The complementarity of cooperative and technological competencies: a resource-based perspective, Journal of Engineering and Technology Management, Vol. 18, pp.1-27

Tzokas, N., Saren, M. and Brownlie, D. (1997) G Generating Marketing Resources by Means of R&D Activities in High Technology Firms, Industrial Marketing Management, Vol. 26, pp.331-340

Vaidya, K., Bennett, D. and Liu, X. (2007) Is China's manufacturing sector becoming more high-tech? Evidence on shifts in comparative advantage, 1987-2005, Journal of Manufacturing Technology Management, Vol. 18, No. 8, pp. 1000-1021

deVrandea, V., deJong, J. P. J., Vanhaverbekec, W. and deRochemontd, M. (2009) Open innovation inSMEs:Trends,motives and management challenges, Technovation, Vol. 29, pp. 423-437 van Riel, A. C. R. and Lievens, A. (2004) New service development in high tech sectors A decision-making perspective, International Journal of Service Industry Management, Vol. 15, No. 1, pp. 72-101

Vyas, N., Shelburn, W. and Rogers, D. (1995) An analysis of strategic alliances:forms, functions and framework, Journal of Business & Industrial Marketing, Vol. 10, No. 3, pp. 47-60

Wagner, B. (2003) Learning and knowledge transfer in partnering: an empirical case study, Journal of Knowledge Management, Vol. 7, No. 2, pp. 97-113

Wilson, J. and Hynes, N. (2009) Co-evolution of firms and strategic alliances: Theory and empirical evidence, Technological Forecasting & Social Change, Vol. 76, pp. 620-628

Walton, J. S. and le Guarisco, G. (2007) Structural issues and knowledge management in transnational education partnerships, Journal of European Industrial Training, Vol. 31, No. 5, pp. 358-376

Weinshall, T. D. and Vickery, L. (1987) Entrepreneurs: A Balanced View of their Role in Innovation and Growth, European management journal, Vol. 5, No. 4, pp. 256-267

West, A. (1992) Innovation Strategy Prentice Hall Int. (UK) Ltd

Wöhrl, R., Hüsig, S. and Dowling, M. (2009) The interaction of R&D intensity and firm age: Empirical evidence from technology-based growth companies in the German "Neuer Markt", Journal of High Technology Management Research, Vol. 20, pp. 19-30

Wong, C. (1998) 'Determining Factors for Local Economic Development: The Perception of Practitioners in the North West and Eastern Regions of the UK', Regional Studies, Vol. 32, No.8, pp. 707 -720

Wu, J. and Callahan, J. (2005) Motive, form and function of international R&D alliances: Evidence from the Chinese IT industry, Journal of High Technology Management Research, Vol. 16, pp. 173-191

Xie, F. and Johnston, W. (2004) Strategic alliances: incorporating the impact of e-business technological innovations, Journal of Business & industrial marketing, Vol. 19, No. 3, pp. 208-222

Yahaya, S. and Abu-Bakar, N. (2007) New product development management issues and decision-making approaches, Management Decision, Vol. 45, No. 7, pp. 1123-1142

Yasuda, H. and Iijima, J. (2005) Linkage between strategic alliances and firm's business strategy: the case of semiconductor industry, Technovation Vol. 25, pp. 513-521

Ybarra, C. E. and Turk, T. A. (2009) The evolution of trust in information technology alliances, Journal of High Technology, Management Research, Vol. 20, pp. 62-74

Zehir, C. and Ozsahin, M. (2008) A field research on the relationship between strategic decision-making speed and innovation performance in the case of Turkish large-scale firms, Management Decision, Vol. 46, No. 5, pp. 709-724

Zhang, D. D. and Bruning, E. (2011) Personal characteristics and strategic orientation: entrepreneurs in Canadian manufacturing companies, International Journal of Entrepreneurial Behaviour & Research, Vol. 17, No 1, pp. 82-103

Zineldin, M. and Bredenlow, T. (2003) Strategic Alliance: synergies and challenges A case of strategic outsourcing relationship "SOUR" International Journal of Physical Distribution & Logistics Management, Vol. 33, No.5, pp. 449-464

Bis - Department for innovation and business skills Annual Innovation Report 2010 Accessed on line November 2011

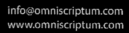

Printed by
Schaltungsdienst Lange o.H.G., Berlin